HOW ROBOT CHANGES BUSINESS ENVIRONMENT

JOHN LOK

ISBN 979-888555659-0

Contents

Preface

Introduction

This book divides three parts. The first part explains online book store competitive effort. The second part explains online travel agent competitive effort.

The first part explains online and offline book shop competition is serious. Book readers have these both channel to choose to buy either electronic book or paper book to study. How can traditional office book shop achieve strategy to compete online book shop ? What are online book shop weaknesses or strengths? What are traditional offline book shop weaknesses or strengths? What is future book publishing development trend? These questions will have suggestions to be given to book publishers to let them to learn more marketing strategies.

The second part aims to explain what strategies will be different between online and offline travel agents . What are the strengths and weaknesses between online and offline travel agents? How can online travel agents win offline travel agents or how can offline travel agents win online travel? Why do travel consumers either choose online travel agents or offline travel agents to help them to arrange travel trips? What factors will change their mind to influence them to choose to buy electronic air ticket or paper air ticket from either offline travel agents or online travel agents? Finally, I shall give my opinions to attempt to answer above questions. It is suitable to any readers who have interest to compare whether online travel agent competitive effort is more or online book store effort is more to develop their online sale market.

Comparison on online book store and online travel agent competitive effort:

In fact, travel agent is one kind of entertainment service industry. Online travel agent can apply online travel website to help travellers to choose any cheap air ticket, hotel, even transportation ticket to pre-book to purchase from internet. Otherwise, book store is one kind of sale service. Online electronic book is one kind of reading method from internet. It give readers feel convenient and easy to read from laptop or mobile phone.

However, I feel online travel agent competition will be difficult to compare to online book store. The reason is because online travel agent lacks individual travel agent explain any journey to let travellers to know by oral. So, some travellers will choose to walk in to travel agent office to enquire travel agent any journeys when they choose any countries to travel. Online travel agent can only provide air ticket price comparison and hotel choices to pre-book service. This is online travel agent weakness. Otherwise, online book store can provide readers to read books from internet, so they do not need to walk in book store to choose book to buy and paper book is heavy, so some readers will prefer to choose electronic to read. Hence, it is the difference between travel psychology and reading to influence why online travellers feel more negative emotion than online electronic book buyer.

This book third part explains how AI office technological development may influence future online tourism and ebook publish more efficient performance. How to predict AI can bring more efficient service performance to online tourism and online publish industry.

Prologue

damage suddence occurrence predicting
- Smart AI Agriculture
- Medicine Delivery to developing countries' patients urgent need
- Assistance to reduce teaching work workload or psychological pressure to teachers in developing countries' schools
- Why does smart phone help developing countries communication ?
- The Positive Impact of Mass Media in Developing Countries
- Why do developed countries need to develop AI
- AI may bring what benefits to developed countries
- How can AI be dangerous when developed countries continue to develop AI to become weapon to replace soldiers?
- Why the recent interest in AI safety ?
- Why do developed countries people need AI ?
   Artificial Intelligence Worker Brings
What Working Environment Influences
- Advantages to robotic bring to working environment
- Disadvantages to robotic bring to working environment

CHAPTER ONE

Online vs offline book shop different development trend

Nowadays, online book ublishing is one kind of popular sale method to global publishing. For example, Amazon publish is as a business model with many potential advantages, relative to a physical operation. It held out the potential of lower book inventing and distribution costs and reduced overhead. Consumers could find the books, they were looking for more easily and a variety book topic choices could be offered for sale. It can accept and fulfill orders from almost any domestic location with equal ease. And most purchasers made on its site would be exempt from sales tax. One Amazon strategy hand, it would have to make its returns and redress processes transparent and reliable, and offer other ways for clients to learn, as much about the book possible before buying. Future online book market development trend, such as Amazon, Barnes & Noble etc. online book shops. How closely would their clients find book ordering, as a substitute for visiting book stores?

In fact, Amazon is global the largest ingle online booksellers and sells many other products. Otherwise, Barnes & Noble, have been market share diminish obviously. In the future, Noble & Barnes both will have their market share diminish continue obviously. There are also many fewer specialty re lowest. Hence, it seems online and offline both publishing methods will be competitive. It brings this questions: What is the trend between online book sale channel, its size relative to offline book sales channel, growth rate and the charcteristcs of reders who by online in the future? How book market's online channels are economically different , due to e-commerce's effects on online book market and supply fundamentals? How an online book sales channel might be expected to change equilibrium market outcomes?

I believe online book channel based sale activity varies considerably on these aspects: Sales in manufacturing printing cost, online sale services and online demand print book sale book topic choices. Such as author online advertising, change more or less sale price, online paper book shipping cost, visa card discount or online book shop member card discount book purchase, what welfares to online book buyers are.

Why readers choose to buy books from internet habit? In tradition, online book buyers habit hope to use the internet to buy. Generally, they have these characteristics: They hope to use the internet to buy electronic books at home, they enjoy to read electronic book from computer, it is in any regular capacity , not ncecessarily to visit book shops to find books to buy and they can search any electronic from internet, electronic book is convenient to read from computer or laptop when they catch transportation or going to anywhere. Usually, internet users are higher income, more educated and younger. It seems that education is a sizeable determinant of who is online, even controlling for income. However, gender does not seems to be a factor in explaining internet use. Moreover, many of book qualitative patterns are seen for online book purchases in general are observed for electronic book products on on demand printing book products in particular.

Predition in future, many of the traditional online products , such as electronic or print on demand books, computer hardware , electronic airline tickets, saw more modest , but still substantial growth. In the future, online sellers trend to be newer online book stores and have less brand or reputation capital to signal or famous brand quality. These factors can create in online book sellers, which also often involve delay. However, there are many reasons for online book purchasing. The most obvious is that readers don't have opportunity where unobservable inferior point of electronic or demand on print book purchases.

● Pricing strategy in online and offline

book retailing

The book price represents consumer behavior on price. On one hand, the model contains two probability fuctions which render consumers' reservation prices for each individual channel. On the other hand, it is based on numerous book distribution which represent probabilities from and to each online or offline book store separate channel. Price strategy of book sale concerns how readers select a particualr book? Both offine and online book information seeking price strategies point out the challenges for information systems development. Hence, book price decision based on readers' age, e.g. children book price will be chealer than adult book price, due to children book content is usually simple and papers page is less. Otherwise, adult book content is more complicated or difficult to understand and page number is more than children book page number. However, online book store disadvantages are that : information system still often fail in supporting the users in causal leisure situations. In order to improve online book search system. Online book stores need to be better understood user strategies and performance and translate them into purposeful features.

A common analysis approach is to compare price and user strategies and interactions in the digital environment with those that occue in similar physical environment. If online bookstores hope to decide more reasonable electronic books or on demand printing books sale prices to compete with offline bookstores. Since, the physical environment (in this particular case bookstores) usually preceds the development of digital environments, processes and strategies from interaction in the physical environment have already stabilized and experiences can be translated into patterns for digital information system development. Thus, some only digital electronic bookstores , such as Amazon publish' disadvantages are : It lacks physical bookstore environment sale experiences. Otherwise, some owning themselves physical book and online book sale environment bookstores, bookstores that can compare only either paper books or electronic books bookstores to predict what the reasonable sale book sale price more easily.

Are these differences between online/digital book discovery environments and offline (neighborhood bookstore) services? Are researching recommendation strategies differences between observable in online and offline book search sessions? In general, interactive users studies based on user interactions in a ISBS developed web-based book discovery information system are aggregated cross multiple researcher groups. In order to provide a realistic book discovery environment, book collection should be large and comparable to other book discovery systems ,such as online book sale. For example, Amazon library book collection is used consisting of approximately 1.5 million books. Each book contains general metadata (title, authors, publisher, publication , year, etc.) subject metadata (classification, code), subject headings , user generated content (Amazon publish user reviewer, library thing user tags).

● How does India book market trend?

Thus, I believe that online or offline bookstore different book research method will also influence readers' preferable book choices, then their choices behavior will influence how many times to find the book easily. If the online or offline readers can find the book topic or author name or contents etc. information easily. Then, the sale chance of the book will increase. Thus, price can increase more. For high population country, e.g. India, China . Does it have more sale chance, due to many people are living in these countries? What us online book store trend in India? Online book can let readers to buy new books and old books from internet, rent or borrow books from internet or access it in the form of e book, e.g. Amazon publish is the big player of online book business in India today. India where dynamic technologies like mobiles are prevalent, e-book readers may soon make into average household. Some of publishing houses which predicted that it would be long journey for e –books to become part of life needs to India readers. Thus, India will be one potential e book market. India is the third biggest market for English books. However, there are challenges of online bookstore in India. IN fact, online book market has changed the way reading consumer use internet for knowledge. Nowadays, people prefer e books are accessible anywhere, any time for creating flexible and secure online bookstore for online bookstores that need to concern to sell their e books to India markets because India readers shall concern visa card payment method where it is safe to pay to read any e books from internet.

Besides, online information searching has touched every field of human life. In the future, it is possible that purchased via mobile are clothing/footwear and e book or on demand print books. Also , due to e book is one kind of popular reading product to be enter India market. Currently, the online book market in India is offering exciting and renewed services to the internet users. India readers can accept to buy old books to read from online sale channel. Thus, India will be one new second hand online book store market to follow developed countries, such as US, UK etc.

● Trend and development on the global book market

Under the influence of internet, new media , social networks. The way in which search to satisfy our needs. Internet is the high technological search method to change at the level of products and services, such as e book (electronic book or demand on print electronic paper book) and online e book rent service , online library e book borrowing services. Thus, in the future, global book market will be popular on concentrating selling e books or online print on demand paper books more than general walk in offline book shop paper books sale only method. Due to, internet changes traditional readers' reading habits to enjoy to read e books from mobiles, laptops, desktops more than paper book reading. Thus, the global book market will be predicted online electronic book sale format more than visiting walk in book ship sale format. The digitalization of information enables us to bring into discussion today contents separated from the physical, materials, paper shapes of the book. Today, books could be found online, read online for free or downloaded as an e book in English or any other language. Practically, the book has changed from paper to electronic book. In until , the internet and the e book , the changes were extremely slow. Today, digitalization produces rapid changes to the entire system of printing, distribution and reading books. Hence, the global book market trend will be the major implication on publishes, distribution, authors and book consumers. The online competition brings major changes to traditional distributors, the bookstores, the author of independent distributors noticeable decreased. The number of big distributors' stores will decrease. For example, Amazon publish is the best known global selling books online. Although, it can sell e books and printing on demand paper books both from internet channel conveniently.

In conclusion, e book market will dominate global online electronic book sale market and the e book publisher number will increase. As the same time, the visiting walk in offline book shop number will decrease, due to readers have accept to use laptops, mobiles to read electronic books from internet channel more than reading paper books. It implies paper book publishers need to change sale method, e.g. adopting internet to sell print on demand paper books, or reducing paper book sale price to attract e book readers to choose to buy paper books to read.

● Web vs School campus book store development trend

Why do students choose to buy textbooks online? What factors motivate students choose online textbooks purchase? Nowadays, many online book retailers, such as Varsity books.com and Bigword.com , Amazon publish.com are now capturing more of the textbook online store market. What is motivating this behavior changes to student market , instead of children story market, entertainment or travel or sport book market etc. topic market. What causes students to choose purchase textbooks online ? Can likelihood to make purchases online by predicted by various social and personal characteristics of consumers? The online textbook purchase growth is allowing online retailers to capture a substantial portion of sales in some sectors. What motivates consumers to shop on the web? But, what if these factors are nor significant , such as better product availability, lower cost, as is that case when comparing on offline textbook purchasing. There is no significant price advantage to buy textbook online, it is there an availability issue, given that textbook can be purchased in the campus store (Foucault et al., 2000).

I shall assume that precious positive online purchase is positively correlated with the likelihood of an individual purchasing textbooks online. Hence, it influences why readers choose to buy textbooks online again. Following , other factor web consumers are likely shop online to save time and/or money, but what of those consumers who shop online when an equally time and cost efficient alternative is present. With regard to textbook purchasing, the time invested in researching for the appropriate books is likely to be similar, regardless of whether the student bookstore or through an online textbook. With regard to textbook purchasing, the time invested in researching from the time invested in searching appropriate books is likely to be similar: regardless of whether the student chooses to shop in the campus bookstore or through an online textbook retailer. If time from purchase until use counts, online textbook shopping could be considered less time efficient than its offline counterpart. Due to the readers need to turn on computer to link to internet to read electronic books or wait the print on demand to buy paper books from the electronic book store web site to wait the paper books to post to the online book buyer's home. Otherwise, offline bookstores can reduce time spending to wait the books to be posted to the buyer's home, after who pay money to take the paper book from the bookstore immediately. So, the non-waiting post book issue is still the text bookstore's strength to attract students to buy.

CHAPTER TWO

Prediction of direction of electronic books future trend

What is future trend of electronic book publishing development? To answer this question, we need to know what benefits of (electronic books) can attribute to human's needs. Nowadays, electronic books (e-books) are one way to enhance the digital library with global 24 hours a day and 7 days a week access to authoritative information, and there enable users to quickly retrieve and access specific research materials easily, quickly and effectively. Evenm some ebooks publishers choose to let readers who can borrow ebooks to online readers to read from online libraries to earn profit. For example, Amazon publisher lets every Amazon readers only pay about US$5 per month. Then, who can borrow unlimited ebooks to read from Amazon publisher private online mPrediction of direction of electronic books future trend

ember library website convenently.

Thus, it is one ebooks online borrowing strategy to compette with offline book stores and public library and school library in publishing industry. Due to offline book stores lack borrowing books services to any walk in readers. However, some countries' publich libraries also have similar ebooks borrowing to read services. An an ebook providers' electonic online libraries, online computer library center has been involved in the selection, catalogue and distribution of ebooks. Library users can able to remotely search, locate and checkout ebooks from the library's online public access catalogues. Thus, ebook publisher will have another public library competitor which can provide similar ebook borrowing service to online ebook readers from public library websites.

It means ebook publishers need to adopt any attractive ebook library sale borrowing service strategy to attract public library readers. However, as with any new opportunity, new challenge utilizes the internet opportunity to deliver new book content is no exception, Integrating ebooks into the digital library has created challenges and opportunities for librarians, publishers and ebooks providers for librarians in this ebook library borrowing service market to earn extra ebook lending service income. Because, online borrowing service library can have ebooks borrowing service, then why online ebook readers need to choose independent ebook publisher individual borrowing book service website to replace traditional public library paper book borrowing service. The reasons possible include that the readers can borrow ebooks to study from ebook publisher individual library borrowing website at home conveniently, but it is possible that they can not find any paper books to borrow from public libraries which are the same ebooks to be borrowed from any one ebook store to read, also ebook publishers can let whose ebook borrowers to borrow unlimited ebooks to read and there are longer extend borrowing ebook return days more than public libraries borrowing book return days and ebook readers have no penalty when they return ebooks too late and they can choose to pay little borrowing ebook charge in the month, if who do not expect to borrow any ebooks in the month, who can choose to stop to pay borrowing ebook charge in the month. Hence, they can choose to continue to borrow unlimited ebook numbers from ebook publishers and they are permitted to return ebooks longer time to compare traditional public libraries. For example, when the ebook reader pay only US$5 ebook library service fee to the ebook publisher in the month , then who can borrow the number of ebook up to 50 maximum number in the month as well as who can return the all ebooks to the ebook library within 60 days, it is longer return days to compare traditional public libraries. If the ebook reader can not return all these ebooks after the return day of 60 day. They can permit to extend more 60 return days. After this another 60 return days, they only need to pay US$5 penalty to the ebook store. Thus, it is one attrative ebook library borrowing service strategy in this competitive book publishing industry.

There is no doubt that the same trends that adopts ebooks and e-readers to US ebook publishing market are having a similar effect in other countries as well, such as Mobile ebook or laptop ebook technical development of reading devices that provide an reading experience similar to that of reading an actual book, the increasing penetration of the internet in all areas of life, which is significantly changing reading patterns and reading behavior. The increasing extent to which ebook or demand on printing book consumers are open to new technological reading trends, for which in particular that availability of attractive mobile devices, such as smartphones, portable games consoles, and MPS players are responsible to ebook reader tools.

Future trend will be that publishers and authors need to build close digital cooperation relationship. Publishers, bookstores and device manufacturers should take the opportunity to provide the market now with innovative ebook publishing products. And authors should explore opportunities for digital distributions and support publishers in their efforts to publish content. Publishers should also design a giving strategy and attractive ebook sale website that attracts customers without undermining the value of content. A well-thought out pricing strategy may also help publishers and content gain new customers, those who would not have purchased a traditional book , but may be inclined to buy an ebook that costs less, offers additional features , and works on a digital device . They already own there, usually the ebook price compares to traditional paper book price which have similar content, ebook price will be cheaper them the similar content of traditional paper book sale price.

In the future, ebook publishers will need to position themselves as content providers, and not just the suppliers of physical books. They will have to make content available on multiples media, in multiple formats, on multiple platforms. This content may not be limited to the text of a book itself, it may also include videos and games. This additional content may lead to incremental revenue.

In fact, the only leisure activities more popular than reading books were watching television, listening to music such the radio and reading newspapers and magazines. Thus, every one should need to choose to enjoy to do what kinds of leisure activities every day. For example, if one person chooses to spend much time to either watch television or listen the music and radio or read newspapers and magazines in the whole day. I believe that he will spend less time to read book in the day. Then, it implies that ebook or paper book readers , the paper book or ebook buyer number will be decrease, due to they spend less time to read or without any reading behavior in the day. Thus, how to persuade every one to feel that reading book habit is attractive or important which can be one factor to influence the paper or electronic book readers, even electronic or paper book buyer number. Thus issue will be an attractive topic to concern for every ebook or paper book publisher on book publishing industry. If these both kind of publishers can persuade any person to feel reading book habit can bring benefits to themselves. They will spend less time to leisure activities. Then, ebook or paper book sale number or ebook borrowing service income will raise in the future. Thus, these both kinds of publishers need to concern how to persuade people to choose to spend some time to read books habitually every day. Consequently, psychological factor will be one important direction to raise book buyer number in publishing industry.

What are the factors to influence sales and
marketing strategies for publishers?

I feel that how to predict book buyers which is driven by book buying experience and the publisher's credibility (loyalty) factors which will influence the any book buyer whose make final decision to buy the book from the publisher. As a publisher, a major goal is to extend whose readership and extend whose readers' influences, but where to start? How do publishers understand and serve diverse readers and decision makers in different countries? Whether can readers find the kind topic of book from publishers only, when find the kind topic of book from the university libraries or public libraries? Hence, due to offline and online publishing industry competition is high, global publishers will need to develop a sales plan to satisfy readers' reading taste. For publishers need to conduct book exhibition activities, visit different author's decision makers to research what who like to write negotiate terms to publish books with individual authors, secure sales and manage orders etc. different regulations of publishing to every author.

I recommend online or offline publisher ought concern how to publish every book before they decide to sel their every electronic book or paper book to any countries' readers. The marketing strategy includes to develop plan every book sale projection, SWOT (strengths, weaknesses, opportunities, or threats) to every book to be published to the country's readers to implement the plan. Book sales program, email communication marketing, lead generation to analyze the results, eg. every book purchasing trends, customer profiles, marketing sementation for every book to follow up and bedrief: Measuring ROI, setting priorities and develops tastics, finally customer needs analysis foe every book sale, it includes GAP analysis, ebook online library visits numbers to experience the ebook and focus groups. The, it is cycle to the develop plan again. Thus, if the publisher can have a better understanding of pricing strategy plan which can create price plan to be strengthed changes or cancelled for every paper book or electronic book sale marketing price strategies. Bringing potentially and disastrous reading experience to readers , this factor can be one good method to increase reader number and book sale price and sale number method. Then, the ebook or paper book publishers can make more accurate ebook or paper book sale price to every sale market, e.g. US or UK which is better book sale market, which kind of book can be the popular to these either market, whether UK readers like to read ebooks more or US readers like to read ebooks more or US readers like to read paper books more or UK readers like to read paper books more. Thus, the ebook or paper book stores can gather these data to analyze whether what every book topic sale price is more accurate to achieve the highest sale number and income.

Consequently, more appealing offerings can be developed to broader every publisher's audience and enhanced whose every publisher's image, segments of reader research, e.g. reader age, book reading taste. This is a measure level of penetration of journals and identity opportunity for growth GAP analysis marketing strategies will be popular methods to future book publishing. Based on first hand, expensive visiting and surveying librarians around the world, examine factors unique to each country and culture and make to recommendations integrate in every publisher's communication plan. For example, ebook trends percentage of ebook spending in online ebook borrowing libraries is a publishing extra income from ebook borrowing readers. It is such one part of the overall electronic book market share income in the electronic book publishing market. In conclusion, internet technological innovation can bring new publishing business chance to ebook development , but it also brings competition to traditional paper book stores. So, paper book stores need have good marketing strategies to win their new ebook competitors.

CHAPTER THREE

The difference between online and offline travel agents

The main cost related factors to offline or online travel agents

Nowadays,many online or offline travel agents have interest to find what the main factors that can affect their strategies to reduce airline costs. The main factors include route structure, type and characteristics of the aircracft, cost of labor and management quality, which will influence whether which airline routes are the most suitable to let online travel agents or offline travel agents to help them to sell paper air tickets or electronic air tickets to attract travel consumption more easily.

Thus, a cost-related strategy is the main important factors to influence travel consumption choice between online or offline travel agents. For example, considering that advantages in costs is an important strategy for carriers to remain in travel transportation market.

The deregulation process of travel markets and increasing opportunities for competition have created excess capacity in many markets that causes lower rates, even with its rising costs. Thus, the travel strategic costs management as well as travel consumers that their behavior under different influences can bring competitive advantages over travel players.

Cost reduction in the travel market -based industry is a very important way of being competitive between offline and online travel agents, when facing travel air ticket prices decreasing for every trip. So reduce to total travel cost, e.g. fuel, maintenance, labor etc. is relevant, but the influence of each component on every total trip cost depends on factors that are related or not to airline operation. For example, some airline can adopt the lowest cost model to sell air tickets from offline or online travel agents which compete for travel passengers with traditional modes as self driving road transport trip in large areas of countries domestic travel market, such as US, UK domestic travel market.

However, the decision about the relevance of one cost is not a simple matter. The effectiveness of reduction of each item that comprises the total cost of airline can change over time, depending on both the business model and the scope of the airline company or online /offline travel agent company as well as external factors.

However, there are three types of competition advantage between online and offline travel market: They are such as agility, differentiation cost and the differentiation may be related to a product of superior quality, higher value f the brand or the company's positive reputation. Such as the online travel agent's providing the different airline cheap air ticket price and kind of trips to provide to travel consumer consumer comparison or the offline travel agent's famous brand or positive reputation to let travel consumers feel travel agents can provide many actual trip package to let them to compare by oral clearly. Thus, the online travel agent's weakness is lack of travel agent individual exploration to let every travel consumer to understand every trip package more clearly.

But online travel agent's strength is it can provdide one website to let travel consumer attempt to compare different trip air ticket and/or hotel price to make personal travel pre-booking decision at home. The another advantage is related to techniques that reduce production cost, making it is possible to offer cheaper air ticket, or hotel room rents, or cheap trip package, than the competition. Such as online travel agent can sell more cheape electronic air ticket price to compare traditional offline travel agent's paper air ticket price.

Finally, agility refers to the speed which the company responds to market demands. For example, if the online travel agent can make statistics to analyze how many online travel consumers to choose to buy which airlines' electronic or paper air tickets, e.g. which airline trip destinations and trips and hotels choices are the most popular attraction to them. Then, the online airline has possible to respond to provide to the most popular airline trips choices, electronic air ticket price comparison choices and hotel rooms prices choices to attract many online travel consumers to enter their online travel websites to choose different airline electronic tickets to buy or pre-book hotel rooms from travel agent websites. Also, if the traditional offline travel agents can attempt to gather every travel consumer's destination trips, hotels , airline paper or electronic ticket prices enquires to make statistics to make which travel trip journeys or destinations and airline paper travel ticket prices are the most popular. Then, it is possible that they can respond to every travel consumer individual demand more to attract whose travel agent choice more easily.

1.2 Airline travel agency AirAsia in the domestic airline low cost strategy

There are three major characteristics of the airline industry namely is product nature, its expenditure structure and its market entry conditions. Airline agent's product is homogeneous or undifferentiated , causing significant competition in airline domestic travel or foreign travel both markets, which are free from regulations and economic barriers. However, high capital and operating expenditure is another important characteristic of the airline industry. Aircrafts, airlines' major capital expenditure are very costly to acquire . For operating expenditures, aviation fuel and labor make up the two major costs in the industry.

Another important characteristic of the airline industry is the conditions for market entry, which differs between international and domestic airline markets . In the international travel market, airline travel agency entry is very difficult as international flights and routes are the results of regotiations between governments . On the other hand, in the domestic and regional travel market, travel agency entry depends on the level of deregulation or liberalisation.

More and more countries, however are opening up their domestic travel markets for more competition. In addition, government plays an important role to regulate the travel markets and existing players may significant influence over now travel agent entrants.

In fact, the mjor factors influence to international or domestic travel consumption increasing numbers are the global economy and safety issues, instead of other different economic factors, such as travel destination choice, electronic air ticket or paper air ticket price, hotel price , the country's political change, e.g. war occurrence, bad weather , e.g. very cold or very hot etc. different factors infuence. Because generally , the world or any region of it is in an economic crisis or depression , the demand for airline services will fall. The late 1990 year Asian financial crisis for example, resulted in minimal increase in the number of worldwide airline passengers incrased only minimally from 1997 to 1998 year. Another factor of influencing the travel passenger number to be decreased, it concerns safety issues are also an important driver of the travel industry, which is subject to very safety standards to influence travel passengers' travel choice to the country. In addition, they are also unexpected safety related events, such as the 11 Sept. 2001 year tragedy in the US, which caused reduction in passengers . The increasing popularity of low cost airlines is the newest trend in the airline industry if which hope many passengers choose to buy whose electronic air ticket or paper air ticket to catch which planes to fly from online travel agent or offline travel agent channels.

The rise of low cost airlines, such as AmericaWest, JetBlue and Airtran in US, Ryanair and EasyJet in Europe and Vigin Blue in Australia. The share of low cost airline strategy is popular in the US and European airline market. For example, the Southwest airline low cost strategy is the basis of most low cost airlines operations. The key of the strategy is to reduce costs when at the same time offering low prices to passengers. History showed that the low cost airline strategy is easy to replicate , but difficult to implement successfully.

However, I suggest airlines need to know what functions which can attract passengers to chose to catch their planes to fly if they expect to rise passenger numbers. For example, the critical function of the Malaysia airline travel is to connect the major towns and remote interior areas within East Malaysia, which has poor road systems and limited availability of other significant means of transportation . In contrast, West Malaysia has more developed and extensive rod and railway systems.

Therefore, airline travel is not the main mode of long distance transportation. It implies Malaysis airline ought concentrate on focusing short distance transportation strategy for passenger beneficial choice function. For example, a new small Malaysia airline serving one or two routes may enter easily. Otherwise, a larger airline servicing multiple routes may be harder to enter Malaysis airline market. It also means access to capital and labor are the major obstacles for new airline entrants to Malaysia airline market. Thus, small airlines into a larger airline is probably more likely to be successful as in Air Asia's case to Malaysia airline market.

Thus, the airline low cost strategy competition positions include very low or minimal pressive from other airline similar service substitute products, low or medium power of airline similar input suppliers. In conclusion, low cost airline strategy is a god method to be attempted to win competitors in airline market.

1.3 How consumers select travel service between online and offline mode in travel industry

Nowadays, the travel industry is operating through two different modes, online and offline respectively. It involves the identification of the competitive strategies adopted by the tour operators. For example, it was found that e-retil travel is platform that is bringing two market forced the demand and supply tour operators and the customers together, and both parties and more inclined towards online mode in near future. Tour operators are gaining by operating at low cost and increasing their business reach when customers get what they desire as per their convenience. For example, many tour operators had promoted tourism destination through website that allow user to use interface for booking transporttion, foreign exchange etc. However, the role of travel operators (agents) should be assisted any airlines to promote their travel package service by internet more easily , such as tourism destination , arrangement of hospitality, restaurants, transportation tools during their trips.

The reasons why consumers choose online travel service include:

Firstly, it is online researching hospitality service. Online travel websites can provide many different accommodation furniture, such as seeking hotel locations, rooms prices comparison, prepaid hotel rooms by visa card payment transaction method, range from luxury five stars deluxe category hotels to small guest houses. The primary need of tourist is to find a place for residing in foreign country or domestic country to ensure whose safety and relaxing needs. Online travel website channel can help whom to find a place , according to his/her needs and paying capacity in the most shorten times.

Secondly, it is online restaurant (food and beverages researching) service. Full service restaurants are divided into two categories, fine dining and casual dining restaurants . Fine dining restaurants are usually located in the premises of luxury hotels, provide high quality food at premium price with good ambience and highly trained professionals. Thus, travel consumers can also compare the different restaurant food price and seek where is the restaurant and find.

What food taste of food supply from the travel agency or travel operator website easily 250 + tour operators are registered with the ministry of tourism (website of tourism ministry) , and the major players in the industry are dealing online and are dominating the travel industry. The major online travel players are Thomas cook, Cox and Kings, make any trips, clear trip, gatra.com and Expedia.

The tour operators whether online or offline offers a large number of services to the tourists including customized package where the customer selects each element of the tour package, specialized tourism package and complete tour guide package.

Nowadays, the tour operational travel (agents) are working through two different modes: offline online . Big brands with luge investment are dealing online and enjoying low cost benefits and huge profit margins. When the small tour operators have their market niche and managing have their market niche and managing their profits by dealing offline.

It is generally prefer offline mode that is the opportunity for small capital investment or employee number for tour operators. But the large scenario is changing as with the usage of internet by the tour operations have given convenience to the customers and now the customers of modern age have started developing preference for online modern. Thus, internet technology change any countries' travel agents or tour operators' air ticket sale method. So, it brings electronic ticket sale method is more popular to compare to traditional travel paper air ticket sale method.

However, online electronic ticket sale method has its disadvantages such as online transaction is unsafe, if the consumer 's name and address and visa card number is stolen to let any internet users to know to be used to buy any products from internet channel easily. Otherwise, traditional walk in offline travel paper ticket sale method is more safe, because the travel consumers can pay cash to the travel agents directly.

However, offline travel agent disadvantages include that the research identified that information communication and technology has very crucial role for tourism industry. Tourist can access any kind of information about tourism destination and tourism products from any part of the world. Tourism comprehends with social media. For example, it was found that (ICT) is bosting up tourism industry. (ICT) helps in searching the location, search for information on tourism products, and e-booking of airline tickets and hotel reservation.

The online travel sale service attraction is that the recent development in the field of information communication and technology and its practical application in tourism and hospitality industry. Generally , online travel sale service must have consumer side and the supplier side.

The decision making prcess of consumer was analyzed and it was found that travel information search and traveller individual electronic ticker pre paid to prebook any plane seat, hotel rooms and restaurants prices comparison to prebook service of traveler individual purchase behavior are corresponding with the usae of (ICT).

1.4 What is the online travel sale service strategy?

The two most important things for travel operators (agents) are online travel marketing and strategic management. Former can enhance business operations. Use of (ICT) develops financial capabilities , however, it depends on management choice, financial condition and position. Some researchers recommended that the usage of IT should not be restricted at operational level, however it should be extended up to senior level and should be used for decision making. Social media is regarded as a platform where the tourists and travel operators/agents (suppliers) of tourism industry cross each other. Thus, the role of social media has been directed for future research in tourism industry. Hence, it seems online travel sale service has these features to attract travel consumers to choose to use this online mode to buy electronic air ticket. Such as, airline electronic air ticket price comparison, pre-booking plan seats to avoid full seats flights to delay consumer individual trip plan, pre-booking hotel rooms and prices comparison as well as prebooking restaurant seats and food price and taste comparison, travel destination easy search. Otherwise, these features to attract travel consumers to choose to walk in to travel agents to buy paper air ticket directly. They include: safe cash or visa card payment to avoid personal information is stolen by website payment channel, e.g. via card number, address, name , birth date personal information. Also the travel consumer can enquire any questions from the travel agent and gets individual feedback from the travel agent by oral before who ensure to choose to buy which kind of travel package for whose travel destination. In special, when the travel consumer has much time to spend to enquire any travel trip question, walk in travel agent is the best enquire methods to let the travel consumer to know the trip information clearly.

CHAPTER FOUR

Online/offline travel operators (agents) marketing strategies

Offline walk in travel unique segment service strategy

Nowadays, online and offlce travel operators competitions are serious. In fact, tourism marketing , there will be more need for online travel operators in the future, due to online travel sale service is popular to be accepted by online travel consumers. Thus, I recommend walk in offline travel agents need to concentrate on focusing some unique travel service to attract new or old travel consumers if who hope to survive.

I recommend that they can focus on specific specialized services, such as travel consultation (specialization) hypothesizing that systematic differences exist between the usage of travel agents for different travel contexts and travel agents can survive if they focus on specific segments of the market, such as older travelers (segmentation; hypothesizing that systematic differences exist between the usage of travel agents depending on the personal characteristics of travellers). The unique travel needs include: specific services related to package holidays, transport services, beach on city holidays, as well as destinations travellers are not familiar with.

I shall give my opinions to provide insight into alternative strategies for travel agencies in a matured travel market with a high internet penetration as below:

The internet online travel sale service is a reality of popular to let travel consumers to feel convenient to pre-book air seat, hotel rooms , air electronic ticket prices comparison. In order to make final purchase decision very easily in the shortest time. Consequently , it has penetrated the decision making process of travel to attract them to choose to buy electronic air ticket, prebooking hotel rooms or restaurant seats from online travel agent channel more than walk in offline travel agent channel. This is especially true in the tourism business where consumption to consume (booking) and the purchase-related information search (Bieger & Lasesser 2004; Crotts 1998).

In fact , apply website to provide travel sale method has these good consequence. From travel operator (agent) supplier's perspective, the success potential derived from operating a website consist of lower distribution costs, higher revenues and a larger potential market share (due to the ubiquitous access). From traverler's perspective, the internet allows direct communication with tourism suppliers facilitatinf requests for information and allowing services and travel related products, e.g. prebooking hotel rooms, restaurant seats , electronic or paper air tickets, travel trip arrangement package products to be purchased at any time and any place from online travel agents /operators conveniently.

Offline / online travel agency (operator) business depends on earn commissions on behalf of airlines. Thus, offline walk in travel agency (operator) business model that would extend existence as a booking agency (thus focusing on consultation and interpersonal contact) strategy.

As a matter of fact, commission -cutting , which began in the US well ahed of Europe, has had a profound effect specially on business travel agents . Consequently , many of them have re-invented themselves as " travel managers", instead of selling tickets and making arrangements, they charge consultancy fees for reducing the amounts client companies spend on travel (Daneshku, 1999).

2.2 Systematic differences strategy applies to offline walk in travel agent

Thus, I recommend systematic differences strategy can be applied offline walk in travel agent (operator). It means that walk in travel agents could reorient their offline walk in travel agent business to focus on contexts that are less substitutable by other channels and media . Factors hypothetically attributing to the delineation of travel contexts include: helping travellers to choose best travel destinations, helping travellers to attempt to find the number of previous trips (indicating the familiarity with a destination) for their travel reference, helping them to find the cheapest, the most convenient and the most close transportation to ctch during their trips, helping them to find the different types of accommodation and rooms price comparison , nature/type of the trip comparison , arrangement of time of booking (as indicator of spontneous / planned travel) nd helping them to budget overall travel expenditure .

Systematic differences in travel agent use exist in dependence of personal (characteristics with with tourists. Walk in offline travel agents could benefit from a travelling client segmentation strategy and customize and target their services to those travellers that are most likely to be and remain their customers.

Factors hypotheticlly attributing to the traveller segment include: travel expenditure per day, useful travel information as indicator for perceived risk and socio-demographic (age, gender, highest completed and education, professional positions) . Generally, the role of walk in offline travel agent with regard to the travel infrrmation search and booking behavior have take an incoming perspective. Such as looking at visitors from different travel markets at a similar destinations. The comparison of central importance in determining whether specialization of travel contexts or market segments is the more promising strategy for walk in offline travel agents.

However, travel package tours strategy must b offline walk in travel attraction . Due to some walk in travellers target segmentation market has still needs. Generally, this travel package tours of travel segmentation consumer who like to enquire the travel agents to concern what the hotel rooms price are the cheapest to provide to them to live, what transportation tools the travel agent can arrange to them to catch anywhere the country destination, the travel agent can provide them to visit during their tour journey. Thus, the travel trip package service is still popular need to offline walk in travel agent (operator). This market is only belonged to offline walk in travel agents (operators) nowadays.

2.3 Service fees and commission cuts strategy

The reduction or removal of airline commission continues to challenge travel agencies' profitability It is crucial to understand what trends travel agencies need to be aware of to ensure how to profitability and increase travel agencies' revenues with service-fee models.

Service fees are not only a way to compensate for the loss of airline commission but also a way to generate new revenue sources for travel agencies that guarantee their long term profitability. Many travel agencies are expanding their service fee models, both in terms of the mounts changed and the number of service to airline.

However, if travel agent charge too much service fee to exceed the general airline travel market service fee reasonable or standard level. It will influence many airlines do not choose to find the travel agent to help them to sell air tickets. Travel agents apply fees most often for airline related services. They charge differentiated fees depending on the destination, type of reservation (e.g. frequent flyer), number of tickets sold or type of airline (e.g. full service versus).

However, service fee increases can raise customer loyalty and satisfaction. It won't reduce client numbers or result in a lose in clients.. The reason is that service fees can be tailored to suit individual customer. This helps travel agencies target their clients, with tailored services based on their past purchasing patterns and identity services for which clients' willingness to pay is greater , such as trip planning identity service for which pay , such as hotel only or special promotion.

To revenue mix for travel agencies is increasingly shifting to service fes as airlines have lowered or cut commissions. Successful travel agencies in many European countries are fast adopting, and constantly upgrading , their service fee schemes. Thus, it seems reasonable service fee level is one important factor to influence travel agents and airlines good relationship. In fact, even travel agents raise service fee, it won't influence travel consumer number to be reduced , even they raise air ticket price. It they can provide the informations concerning the reasonable hotel rooms prices and food quality comparison to satisfy travel consumers' living arrangement or helping them to find the reasonable restaurants' food prices and where are their location arrangement or providing the reasonable airlines' electronic air tickets or paper air tickets sale service, even arrangement any high entertainment quality of travel destination trips to let travel consumers to feel satisfactory.

However, I believe the raise air ticket price factor won't influence the travel consumer number to be decreased. Any offline or online travel agents will encounter this crisis. By cutting travel agents' commission. Airlines decreased their dependence on travel agencies as a distribution channel. In fact, three key variable factors will influence travel agents' commission income to be decreased. They include below:

● The unsustainable or no change financial losses by airlines , due to the growth of low cost carriers, leading to an increase in the number of bankruptcies.

● No negative consequences from previous commission cuts: airline had progressively lowed the commission payments.

● No effective resource for travel agencies to satisfy airlines needs.

● The appearance of now airlines and air routes to provide to travel agencies to fall down air ticket price to attract consumers' choices, due to who don't feel to spend much money to go to this new air routes or catch new airline plans , whether these new air routes are excite to entertainment or whether they are safe planes to catch.

● An increase in the number of bankruptcies to cause travel comsumption desire to be reduced.

● New competition forced down air fares.

● The necessity to cut production costs, especially with low cost meaning low production costs and low fares, even if the two are closely linked.

2.4 Internet negative influences to travel agents

Although, on the one hand, internet creates offline travel agents to use websites to help them to sell electronic air ticket or travel related products, such as prebooking hotel rooms , restaurants, transportation tools etc. travel service. However, on the other hand, internet also brings travel agencies competitive disadvantage with regad to suppliers' direct websites , when airlines are able to control seat availability and prices. Indeed internet cause the decision is made by the airlines to reduce and/or eliminate travel agency commission has led them to use technology that many of their distrust or are not inclined to use, and to compare prices and travel schedules constantly.

As a result of this travel sale service environment, traditional offline travel agencies are at a competitive disadvantage with regard to online travel agencie and to airline carriers, which have developed their own direct websites where they are able to control seat availability and prices.

Nevertheless, travel agents' pay programmes remain. From some airlines, travel agents receive negotiated incentive commission closely linked to their performance as incentive . However, airlines still need travel agents' assistance to help them to promote air tickets to sell, due to travel agents can provide trip packages, transportation tools, prebooking hotel rooms, restaurants and air tickets arrangement and they can give any enquiries to every individual travel consumer. It is free charge travel professional enquiry service for travel agency's competitive features.

Consequently, how agencies can reduce their reliance on airline commission payments. I recommend these following strategic options to them to apply as below:

● Streamlining operations, controlling staff costs, when ensuring the client feels as little impact as possible.

● Expanding or moving into the leisure business, where commissions on ono-air products remain high (cruise, hotel, railway travel)

● Specializing in geographic areas or becoming niche players for specific leisure products, e.g. destination weddings, student travel group cultural travel, cruises only, cruise and railway travel etc.

● (d) establishing a service fee driven business model.

2.5 Concentrating on business travel marketing strategy

The certain characteristics to the business travel market allowed this sector to adapt more easily to the disappearance of commission. Business travel systems have always had different relationship with different customers. They usually have long term buyer relationships, set up long before the commission cap. Some of them quickly renegotiated their contracts to include a transaction or management fee, knowing that the majority of these fee arrangements are specific the need of the client.

The reasons why airlines reduce commission to paid to travel agents. They include petrol costs increasing, e.g. indirect and by pass the established distribution chain by developing airlines' their own websites; reducing or removing commission paid to travel agencies. Consequently, the decision to cut travel agencies' commission clearly shows that airlines wanted to decrease their reliance and dependence on travel agencies as a distribution channel. Thus, the internet appears to be an efficient and cost-effective distribution channel. Also, by creating airlines' own websites and setting directly to their clients, airlines are also to control seat availability to their clients and prices to their websites.

2.5.1 What an e-commerce strategy is used by internet travel websites?

Nowadays, the commercial use of electronic travel ticket travel is common, the most purchased online products include, for example, the name brands in online travel Epedia.travel .com and cheap tickets have been or are being integrated in large online travel firms.

Generally, online travel websites apply these strategies to attract travel consumers as below:

Firstly, shopping mall strategy, means to conduct a comprehensive factors for e-commerce. The online service provider needs to organize catalogs of services, take orders through their websites, accept payments securely, send service or related document, such as airline tickets to consumers and manage client data , such as client profiles.

Secondly, portal strategy, portal websites , such as yahoo give visitors the chance to find almost everything , they are working for in one place. Websites , such as Altavista.com and yahoo.com provide users with a shopping page that links them to many sites carrying a variety of products. Once a client is familiar with a website, who will be more likely to use the online service.

Thirdly, pricing strategy, low price is as a major competitive weapon. It includes a comparison pricing on discount price or price negotiation to let online travel consumers to get the best electronic travel ticket price choice to buy any airline tickets.

2.5.2 Travel agents vs online booking: Tackling the shortcomings and strengths

Consequently, however, one travel consumer who chooses either online booking sale service or traditional walk in offline travel agent to enquire travel service. These both of travel sale methods have shortcomings also. Such as it is possible that online electronic travel ticket purchase has personal data ,e.g. visa card, name, birth data, address, which will be stolen by online crime internet users more easily, who can not enquire any travel questions to get clear travel information concern whose travel destination package service choice or hotel room choice or transportation tool or restaurant choice and airline choice by travel agent. Also, it is possible that walk in travel agent paper travel ticket purchase shortcomings include that the travel consumer can not check any airlines' seat and pre book hotel room or transport tool or restaurant in the shorten time if who needs to fly immediately. Thus, it seems that online travel agent's client group is business travel intention, who does not need to enquire travel agent and has desire to per book airline seat in the short time. Otherwise, the offline walk in agent's client group is entertainment intention , who need to walk in to travel agent to enquire whose travel package and has no desire to pre book airline seat in the short time. Thus, online travel agent ought concentrate on design good travel package for the business travel consumers. Otherwise, offline travel agent ought concentrate on design good travel package for the entertainment travel consumers. Thus, they can have themselves unique travel target package to adopt to their different travel need. Such as business travel consumers need to live cheap and comfortable hotels, catching cheap and fast transportation tools in their business trips, eating in cheap and good taste food in restaurant and spending the less time to catch the airline plan to arrive the destination and cheap and comfortable business class plan seat. Such as entertainment travel consumers need the travel agent can help them to design cheap and enjoyable travel package, includes living comfortable hotel room, exciting and enjoyable trip, good taste food and railway, travel bus, cruise and plane provision in trip.

In conclusion, In fact, tourism is a quite unique area of business in a sense that is a travel sale service product and it can't be observed or manipulated through direct experience prior to purchase . Instead clients have to purely rely on indirect or virtual experience. Thus, every online or offline travel agent ought attempt to design different travel package to attract every business traveler or entertainment traveller trip need because every traveler will have personal unique trip need in this competitive travel sale service market in the future.

Reference

Bieger. Th., and Ch. Laesser (2004). " Information sources for travel decisions: Toward a source process model," Journal of travel reserch, 42(4): 357-371.

Daneshku, S. (1999). " Unwived travel agents unworried bi internet, " Financial Times , London. June 16, 1999:10.

Foucault, B. Lery, N. Rifkin, A. & Silfies , 2000.
" Comparision of textbook prices by retailer and by college" working paper. Cornell University, Ithaca, Ney.

CHAPTER FIVE

AI technology how is applied to online office working environment

Artificial intelligence bank service working environment

Focus on outcomes not technology.Artificial Intelligence: Waiting to be unleashed? The Insider Column - When Digital Transformation misses. Are you meeting the demands of the new digital consumer? Will your legacy mindset compromise your digital competitiveness? Can artificial intelligence create online remote office new business service market in global ?

The Future of Artificial Intelligence In The Workplace:

Is AI going to displace workers or come as a benefit to them?

Is AI going to displace workers or come as a benefit to them? Getty

Smart technologies aren't just changing our homes; they're edging their way into their numerous industries and are disrupting the workplace. Artificial Intelligence (AI) has the potential to improve productivity, efficiency and accuracy across an organization – but is this entirely beneficial? Many fear that the rise of AI will lead to machines and robots replacing human workers and view this progression in technology as threat rather than a tool to better ourselves.

With AI continuing to be a prominent online office service business to replace human actual office working environment, businesses need to realize that self-learning and black-box capabilities are not the panacea. Many organisations are already beginning to see the incredible capabilities of AI, using these advantages to enhance human intelligence and gain real value from their data. As there is increasing evidence demonstrating the benefits of intelligent systems, more decision-makers in the boardroom are gaining a better understanding of what AI can really offer. Research conducted by EY explains "organizations enabling AI at the enterprise level are increasing operational efficiency, making faster, more informed decisions and innovating new products and services." Can articial intelligent technology create remote office working environment to replace our traditional actual office work environment ? Can we do not need to go to office to work , when any office staffs ,e.g. managers, clerk, etc. they can apply artificial intelligent technology and online technology to work at home, such as remote office working environment ?

The first companies employing AI systems across the board will gain competitive advantage, reduce cost of operations and remove head counts. Whilst this may be a positive from a business perspective, it is obvious why this a worry for those working in roles at risk of displacement. The introduction of these technologies will likely trigger an issue with unions and job security due to the substantial operational changes. Although AI will affect every sector in some way, not every job is at equal risk. PwC predicts a relatively low displacement of jobs (around 3%) in the first wave of automation, but this could dramatically increase up to 30% by the mid-2030's. Occupations within the transport industry could potentially be at much greater risk, whereas jobs requiring social, emotional and literary abilities are at the lowest risk of displacement.

A positive future with artificial intelligence to bring remote online office working environment chance:

Many businesses and individuals are optimistic that this AI-driven shift in the workplace will result in more jobs being created than lost. As we develop innovative technologies, AI will have a positive impact on our economy by creating jobs that require the skill set to implement new systems. 80% of respondents in the EY survey said it was the lack of these skills that was the biggest challenge when employing AI programs.

It is likely that artificial intelligence will soon replace jobs involving repetitive or basic problem-solving tasks, and even go beyond current human capability. AI systems will be making decisions instead of humans in industrial settings, customer service roles and within financial institutions. Automated decisioning will be responsible for tasks such as approving loans, deciding whether a customer should be onboarded or identifying corruption and financial crime.

Organisations will benefit from an increase in productivity as a result of greater automation, meaning more revenue will generated. This thus provides additional money to spend on supporting jobs in the services sector.Due to the vast array of jobs that could be impacted by AI, it is fundamental to address the potential pitfalls of these technologies. Business need to overcome the trust and bias issues surrounding AI by achieving an effective and successful implementation that makes it possible for everyone to benefit.

Governments must ensure that gains from AI are shared widely across society to prevent social inequality between those affected and unaffected by these developments. For example, this could be through increased investment into training. With the additional cost-savings from implementing AI systems, employers should also focus on upskilling their current employees.

To properly leverage the power of AI, we need to address the issue at an educational level, as well as in business. Education systems needs to focus on training students in roles directly associated to working with AI, including programmers and data analysts. This requires more emphasis to be put on STEM subjects (science, technology, engineering and mathematics). Also, subjects centered around building creative, social and emotional skills should be encouraged. Whilst artificial intelligence will be more productive than human workers for repetitive tasks, humans will always outperform machines in jobs requiring relationship-building and imagination. Hence, artificial intelligence will change our world both inside and outside the workplace. Instead of focusing on the fear surrounding automation, businesses need to embrace these new technologies to ensure they implement the most effective AI systems to enhance and compliment human intelligence.

Artificial Intelligence (AI) in Banking working environment
Artificial Intelligence (AI) is a fast-evolving technology, gaining popularity all around the world. Several industries have already adopted AI for various applications, getting better and smarter day by day. In the past few years, the banking sector has also become one of the leading adopters of Artificial Intelligence. Most banks and financial institutions are implementing AI to add more efficiency to their back-office and lessen security risks.

As per Statista, the AI market in the United States is forecasted to reach 7.35 billion U.S. dollars in 2018. Some major applications of AI include classification, image recognition, object identification, and automated geophysical feature detection. Speaking of banking and financial institutions, JPMorgan Chase, Wells Fargo, Bank of America, CitiBank, and other leading U.S. banks have already implemented AI in their systems, helping consumers manage their daily banking needs more efficiently.

AI technology can bring better Customer Support in bank service environment

Several pieces of evidence advocate that the customers willingly prefer self-service options which allow them to chat with a virtual assistant as if it were a live customer representative. Most leading banks have already added virtual assistants to their instant website chatbots, voice response systems, and mobile applications. Artificial Intelligence considers each interaction as a teachable moment, so the chatbots (virtual assistants) keeps getting better while understanding customers. With AI, virtual assistants can deliver better customer support. It also allows sentiment analysis, so the virtual assistant can determine when individuals are getting frustrated and instantly transfer them to a live agent.

Enhanced Banking Services

AI streamlines the banking process while giving customer service a new level of comfortability. It allows banks to meet customers' expectations with comprehensive digital support. With Artificial Intelligence, you can achieve greater precision and accuracy. From cash transfer to bills payment, cards management, and other support, AI can significantly enrich the satisfaction level of your customers. All of these operations can be easily managed through desktops, smartphones, and other mobile devices.

Scam Recognition

With an immense growth of banking fraud, scam recognition and reduction has become challenging for the banking sector. Several banks tried to identify the factors and powerful solutions but couldn't succeed. However, AI makes it easier to detect the factors involved in frauds and support investigators. It improves financial security with advanced fraud prevention tactics. Artificial Intelligence works as a real-time scam solution for the banking sector while handling complex situations and tactics. Based on advanced data crunching, AI can detect fraud by flagging unusual transactions. It also feeds back into the consumer's profile which subsequently builds a secure environment.

Advanced Data Analytics

One of the main advantages of AI is its ability to complete tedious tasks through intricate automation, resulting in better productivity. Based on a machine learning algorithm, AI can quickly consume and process a massive amount of data at an expedited level. The enormous speed brings efficiency to financial services, providing scope for personalized offerings to consumers. What's even more, AI makes faster decisions while carrying out actions quickly. With such advantages, it is nearly obvious that the majority of banks and financial institutions will adopt AI to stay competitive and deliver better customer support. However, several cons are also associated with a machine learning algorithm. As it continues to learn and grow, the decision-making capabilities may create problems in the near future.

Disadvanages of AI in Banking Sector

Artificial intelligence is also expected to massively disrupt banks and traditional financial services. Some of its disadvantages are listed below.

Highly Expensive

Production and maintenance of artificial intelligence demand huge costs since they are very complex machines. AI also consists of advanced software programs which require regular updates to meet the needs of the changing environment. In the case of critical failures, the procedure to reinstate the system and recover lost codes may require enormous time and cost.

Bad Calls

Though Artificial Intelligence can learn and improve, it still can't make judgment calls. Humans can take individual circumstances and judgment calls into account when making decisions, something that AI might never be able to do. Replacing adaptive human behavior with AI may cause irrational behavior within ecosystems of humans and things.

Distribution of Power

There is a constant fear of AI superseding or taking over the humans. Artificial intelligence can give a lot of power to the few individuals who are controlling it. Hence, AI carries the risk and takes control away from humans while dehumanizing actions in several ways.

Unemployment

Replacement of the workforce with machines can lead to wide-reaching unemployment. Moreover, if the use of AI becomes rampant, people will be highly dependent on the machines and lose their creative power. Unemployment is a socially undesirable issue. Individuals with nothing to do can lead to the devastating use of their minds. Be it banking or any other sector; Artificial intelligence can effectively increase the unemployment rate.

Artificial Intelligence delivered to wrong hands can turn out to be a serious threat to humankind. If individuals start thinking destructively, they can generate havoc with these advanced machines. The challenges introduced by the emergence of artificial intelligence revolve around several things. However, AI is a right balance of skill and emotions which is continually growing. Artificial intelligence provides banks, financial institutions, and tech companies with significant competitive advantages. Nevertheless, it can completely transform the financial sector and make it faster, but this will only be possible if the financial industry can manage the security risk of systems based on AI.

What does artificial intelligence mean for the bank service office workers?

With all these new artificial intelligence use cases comes the question of whether machines will force humans into obsolescence. The jury is still out: Some experts vehemently deny that artificial intelligence will automate so many jobs that millions of people find themselves unemployed, while other experts see it as a pressing problem.

"The structure of the workforce is changing, but I don't think artificial intelligence is essentially replacing jobs in bank service working environment. It allows us to really create a knowledge-based economy and leverage that to create better automation for a better form of life. It might be a little bit theoretical, but I think if you have to worry about artificial intelligence and robots replacing some bank service jobs, e.g. bank security, bank enquiry service,. But, AI can not replace bank counter service staffs to do saving or withdrawing money transfer tasks when any customers prepare to save money or withdraw money in bank counters. As this technology develops, the AI bank service will see new startups, numerous saving or withdraw transactions from consumer won't be raise more easily.

AI to Banking and Finance industry

The banking and finance industry plays a major role in our lives. I mean the world runs on money and banks are essentially the gatekeepers that regulate that flow. Did you know that the banking and finance industry heavily relies on artificial intelligence for things like customer service, fraud protection, investment, and more? A simple example is the automated emails that you receive from banks whenever you do an out of the ordinary transaction. Well, that's AI watching over your account and trying to warn you of any fraud.

AI is also being trained to look at large samples of fraud data and find a pattern so that you can be warned before it happens to you. Also, when you hitch a little snag and chat with bank's customer service, chances are that you are chatting with an AI bot. Even the big players in the finance industry use AI to analyze data to find the best avenues to invest money so they can get the most returns with the least risk. That's not all, AI is poised to play an even bigger role in the industry as major banks across the world are investing billions of dollars in the AI technology and we all will observe its effects sooner than later

How AI influences our daily working life in any office working environment

Can AI bring only disadvantages? If AI can bring disadvantges, what are its disadvantages to any working environment ?The entire tech world is debating the consequences of artificial intelligence and the part AI is going to play in shaping our future. While we might think that artificial intelligence is at least a few years away from causing any considerable effects on our lives, the fact remains that it is already having an enormous impact on us. Artificial intelligence is affecting our decisions and our lifestyles every day. Don't believe me? I shall indicate some product examples how AI anticipates which can influence our working culture in any office environment.

Examples of how Artificial Intelligence assistance to office working environment may include as below:

1. Smartphones

Smartphones have become the most indispensable tech product that we own today and we use it almost all the time. Well, if you are using a smartphone, you are interacting with AI whether you know it or not. From the obvious AI features such as the built-in smart assistants to not so obvious ones such as the portrait mode in the camera, AI is impacting our lives in every day office working environment.

In fact, the two examples that I provided that our working world of AI and how it is effecting our working lives. Firstly, there are the obvious AI elements which most of us have some knowledge about. For example, when you are using a smart assistant in office, whether it's Google Assistant, Alexa, Siri, or Bixby, you more or less know that these assistants are based on AI. However, when we are using a feature such as the portrait mode effect while shooting a picture, we never consider that AI might be behind that too. Have you ever thought how the Google Pixel phones or iPhones can capture such great portrait shots? The answer is artificial intelligence.

So, when any office workers need to find any knowledge to solve their working problem immediately in any offices. They may apply AI smart phone tools to help them to apply online channel to search any new knowledge to attempt to solve their working problem in possible, when their computers have none any computers in offices.

Now more and more manufacturers are including AI in their smartphones with big chip manufacturers including Qualcomm and Huawei producing chips with built-in AI capabilities. The AI integration is helping in bringing features like scene detection, mixed and virtual reality elements, and more. AI is going to play an even major role in the coming years. We are already seeing the huge emphasis on AI with the latest Android and iOS updates. Features like app actions, splices, and adaptive battery in Android Pie and Siri shortcut and Siri suggestions in iOS 12 are made possible with AI. So, next time if any office workers think AI is not effecting them, take out your smartphone to replace computers to find any knowledge to help you to solve any tasks problems immediately in offices.

2. Social Media Feeds

If you are thinking that smart cars don't personally effect you as they are still not in your country or city, well, how about something which you use on a daily basis. Even if you are living under a rock, there's a high probability that you are tweeting from underneath it. If Twitter's not your choice of poison, maybe it's Facebook or Instagram, or Snapchat or any of the myriad of social media apps out there. Well, if you are using social media, most of your decisions are being impacted by artificial intelligence. So, any office workers may apply AI to help them to gather any new information to solve any difficult task problems , if their managers can not assist them to solve any sudden tasks problem, they are encountering to need to solve any working complex tasks problem internet social media in any any office working environment immediately.

From the feeds that office staffs can see in their working timeline to the notifications that you receive from these apps, everything is curated by AI. AI takes all your past behavior, web searches, interactions, and everything else that you do when you are on these websites and tailors the experience just for you. The sole purpose of AI here is to make the apps so addictive that you come back to them again and again, and I am ready to place a bet that AI is winning this war against you.

3. Online Ads Network

One of the biggest users of artificial intelligence is the online ad industry which uses AI to not only track user statistics but also serve us ads based on those statistics. Without AI, the online ad industry will just fail as it would show random ads to users with no connection to their preferences what so ever. AI has become so successful in determining our interests and serving us ads that the global digital ad industry has crossed 250 billion US dollars with the industry projected to cross the 300 billion mark in 2019. So next time when any product developers are going online and seeing ads or product recommendation, know that AI is impacting to any new products advertisement method more efficiently.

4. AI can be any office security

While we can all debate the ethics of using a broad surveillance system, there's no denying the fact that it is being used and AI is playing a big part in that. It is not possible for humans to keep monitoring multiple monitors with feeds from hundreds if not thousands of cameras at the same time, and hence, using AI makes perfect sense. With technologies like object recognition and facial recognition getting better and better every day, it won't be long when all the security camera feeds are being monitored by an AI and not a human. While there's still time before AI can be fully implemented such as security in any offices, this is going to be our future.

5. Smart Keyboard Apps

Smart Keyboard Apps. Granted, not everyone loves dealing with on-screen keyboards. However, they have become far more intuitive, allowing users to type comfortably and faster. What has probably proved to be a catalyst for them is the integration of AI. The smart keyboard apps keep a tab on the writing style of a user and predict words and emojis accordingly. Thus, typing on the touchscreen has become faster and more convenient. Not to mention, artificial intelligence also plays a vital role in pin-pointing misspellings and typos. So, any office workers can apply smart keyboard apps to help their to raise typing efficiency and reduce wrong typing word in error when they need to type any document in offices.

6. E-Commerce

` AI-driven algorithms have kind of given the much-needed impetus to e-commerce to provide a more personalized experience. According to several reports, its usage has vastly increased sales and also played a good part in building loyal relationships with customers. Thus, companies take advantage of AI to deploy chatbots to collect pivotal data and also predict purchases to create a customer-centric experience. Yet to come across this shift of strategy? Just spend some time with sites like Amazon and eBay and you will soon get to know how fast the landscape is changing around you – for the better! So, Ai can help any businesses to achieve e-commerce sale channel more easily.

7. Smart Email Apps

In any office working environment, if you still find your inbox cluttered with too many unwanted messages, chances are pretty high that you are still stuck with an old school email app. You heard it right! Modern email apps like Spark make the most of AI to get rid of spam messages and also categorize emails so that you can quickly access the important ones. What's more, they also offer smart replies based on the messages you receive to help you reply to any email quickly. The "Smart Reply" feature of Gmail is a great example of this. It uses AI to scan the text of the email and provides you with contextual answers. So, AI can help any office staffs to know who had sent any message from email and respond their email immediate , when AI can help any offices to avoid to receive any email spam rubbish email message in any time, even after working hours, it means that AI is working to help any office staffs to avoid to receive any email spam rubblish message in any time. So, when they go to office to work, even they go home after working hours. They can know whether what the important email messages are sent to their office email in boxes any time. Then, they can send email to respond their customers' enquires any time. So, AI can help any office workers can have chance to work at homes.

The Future of Artificial Intelligence In The Workplace
Smart technologies aren't just changing our homes; they're edging their way into their numerous industries and are disrupting the workplace. Artificial Intelligence (AI) has the potential to improve productivity, efficiency and accuracy across an organization – but is this entirely beneficial? Many fear that the rise of AI will lead to machines and robots replacing human workers and view this progression in technology as threat rather than a tool to better ourselves.

With AI continuing to be a prominent buzzword in 2019, businesses need to realize that self-learning and black-box capabilities are not the panacea. Many organisations are already beginning to see the incredible capabilities of AI, using these advantages to enhance human intelligence and gain real value from their data. As there is increasing evidence demonstrating the benefits of intelligent systems, more decision-makers in the boardroom are gaining a better understanding of what AI can really offer. Research conducted by EY explains "organizations enabling AI at the enterprise level are increasing operational efficiency, making faster, more informed decisions and innovating new products and services."

Today In: Cybersecurity

The first companies employing AI systems across the board will gain competitive advantage, reduce cost of operations and remove head counts. Whilst this may be a positive from a business perspective, it is obvious why this a worry for those working in roles at risk of displacement. The introduction of these technologies will likely trigger an issue with unions and job security due to the substantial operational changes. Although AI will affect every sector in some way, not every job is at equal risk. PwC predicts a relatively low displacement of jobs (around 3%) in the first wave of automation, but this could dramatically increase up to 30% by the mid-2030's. Occupations within the transport industry could potentially be at much greater risk, whereas jobs requiring social, emotional and literary abilities are at the lowest risk of displacement.

A positive future with artificial intelligence

Many businesses and individuals are optimistic that this AI-driven shift in the workplace will result in more jobs being created than lost. As we develop innovative technologies, AI will have a positive impact on our economy by creating jobs that require the skill set to implement new systems. 80% of respondents in the EY survey said it was the lack of these skills that was the biggest challenge when employing AI programs. It is likely that artificial intelligence will soon replace jobs involving repetitive or basic problem-solving tasks, and even go beyond current human capability. AI systems will be making decisions instead of humans in industrial settings, customer service roles and within financial institutions. Automated decisioning will be responsible for tasks such as approving loans, deciding whether a customer should be onboarded or identifying corruption and financial crime. Organisations will benefit from an increase in productivity as a result of greater automation, meaning more revenue will generated. This thus provides additional money to spend on supporting jobs in the services sector.

How to take advantage of AI to any offices

Due to the vast array of jobs that could be impacted by AI, it is fundamental to address the potential pitfalls of these technologies. Business need to overcome the trust and bias issues surrounding AI by achieving an effective and successful implementation that makes it possible for everyone to benefit. Governments must ensure that gains from AI are shared widely across society to prevent social inequality between those affected and unaffected by these developments. For example, this could be through increased investment into training.With the additional cost-savings from implementing AI systems, employers should also focus on upskilling their current employees.

To properly leverage the power of AI, we need to address the issue at an educational level, as well as in business. Education systems needs to focus on training students in roles directly associated to working with AI, including programmers and data analysts. This requires more emphasis to be put on STEM subjects (science, technology, engineering and mathematics). Also, subjects centered around building creative, social and emotional skills should be encouraged. Whilst artificial intelligence will be more productive than human workers for repetitive tasks, humans will always outperform machines in jobs requiring relationship-building and imagination. Artificial intelligence will change our world both inside and outside the workplace. Instead of focusing on the fear surrounding automation, businesses need to embrace these new technologies to ensure they implement the most effective AI systems to enhance and compliment human intelligence

How AI can help office workers to do tasks more easily

Companies are currently spending big on artificial intelligence and machine learning initiatives to the tune of $12 billion, but estimates put that figure as high as $57.6 billion by 2021, according to the International Data Corporation (IDC). With such massive shifts, the focus is usually on what we might lose, but it shouldn't be. A recent report on the future of work from the McKinsey Global Institute suggests that while only about 5% of jobs can be completely eliminated by automation, the rise of AI requires workers to beef up both technical and soft skills in order to stay competitive.

What's seldom discussed is how AI can revolutionize our jobs. It's now possible to pinpoint peak productivity for a single day, improve communication in meetings (even before people ever work together face to face), or even teach you to be a better leader, all thanks to AI platforms. I shall indicate these advantages to bring any office benefits from AI assistance as below:

1. AI can help any companies to get better to hire the best applicants
AI has the greatest potential to change the way companies find candidates, according to Alexander Rinke, cofounder and CEO of Celonis. The company's process-mining technology helps businesses to understand the areas where automation can help humans, he says. In HR departments, Celonis can help identify how fast workers come and go, the cost per hire, and which positions take the longest to fill. AI helped enable one customer's ability to identify bottlenecks in recruitment and reduced process costs internally by 30% as well as get them hired more quickly, he says.
Crafting a resume has never been easier, nor has landing an interview. Another example is how recruitment software provider iCIMS, in partnership with Google, is helping job seekers find jobs directly through the search engine, thanks to Google's AI and machine learning capabilities. Susan Vitale, iCIMS's chief marketing officer says that in addition to reducing the number of expired job postings, machine learning is underlying a private beta program of Google's Cloud Jobs Discovery model. "For a candidate searching for, say, a CTO role, Cloud Job Discovery will serve up CTO positions as well as jobs with titles that are similar, but not verbatim, such as chief technology officer or chief technical officer," says Vitale. This model also allows for conceptual search results, such as serving up job listings for cashiers, sales associates, and store associates when someone searches for one versus just only showing jobs that exactly match the keyword search criteria, she adds.
2. AI can help any office workers to raise much more productive efficiencies
John Furneaux, CEO and cofounder of Hive, says predictive analytics will help us better understand how we work. "It can tell us just about everything we want to know about teams and collaboration, for example, if men or women get more done in the afternoon, and if summer Fridays are a myth," he says. (Everyone thinks summer Fridays aren't productive, but in reality there's no difference between those and other Fridays during the year—productivity is equally low.)
Using a data set of over 30,000 completed actions across Hive workspaces, Furneaux says they were able to identify some notable trends in productivity. For example, men were far more productive early in the day, with a sharp decline in the afternoon, while women had a slower start to the day but were far more productive in later hours than their male counterparts. And analyzing chat messages revealed that women appear to

complete more tasks when chatting, suggesting they use communication as a key tool to completing work. Similarly, Nintex Hawkeye analyzes data on business processes by types, users, roles, and departments to see who's doing the work and how long it takes them to do it. Management can monitor and analyze those metrics in real time.

3. AI can help any managers to make the most fair compensation and eliminate wage gaps to every staffs

Tanya Jansen, cofounder of the compensation management platform beqom, says that AI and predictive analytics can eliminate unconscious bias from compensation. Jansen says that AI based on a variety of rules including education, experience, certifications, and more can make compensation more fair and help businesses move closer to closing pay gaps. "Specifically, AI can help solve gender pay gaps and the CEO-to-worker pay gap, in which pay ratios of Fortune 500 companies range from 2:1 at the low end to nearly 5000:1 at the high end," she says. Additionally, the use of AI-driven compensation technology to make pay more fair can mitigate the risk of employee turnover, which costs businesses as much as 33% of a worker's annual salary to replace them.

4. AI can help any office staffs to arrange better meetings

Augmented Reality (AR) is still in its infancy, but AI and machine learning are the core components that make it work. As such, Christa Manning, the vice president and solution provider research leader at Bersin, Deloitte Consulting LLP, says that AR can help workers find the right information, in the right place, at the right time to make the best decisions wherever they may be working. For example, as more companies adopt video meetings and collaborative workspaces, it's likely we'll begin to see HR-curated information like talent profiles and work styles layered over interactions through AR."Imagine being in a video conference with a colleague and having direct insight into their communication style, seeing tips on how to best interact with them or reminders of what needs to be discussed. SO, AI can help any organizations to conclude or find the best methods to solve any problems after their every discussion in any meetings.

How AI is improving onboarding and training. AI coaching tools first learn by observing how different employees conduct specific tasks. Then these tools can walk new employees through how to complete those tasks—or even coach existing employees on how to do things more effectively or efficiently. Chorus is a great example of this technology. It analyzes sales calls while they happen, offering tips to help sales reps manage the cadence of meetings and use the most effective messaging. It also records all sales calls and compiles statistics for each sales rep, providing everyone with the tools they need to help them close more deals and conduct more effective calls. Another example is Cogito, a tool that combines AI with behavioral science to help customer service employees provide better phone support. It monitors calls for voice signals, providing real-time suggestions to representatives on how to improve the conversation.

5. AI can help any managers to be better leaders

Indiggo, a platform powered by a proprietary AI tool called "indi," functions as a brain that has consumed all the knowledge the company has gathered in its 15 years of operation. It also uses an algorithm to provide an estimate of how much time is wasted by a company by analyzing the size of its management team. Then it taps their calendars to see how they spend their time, and walks individual managers through a type of Q&A to make sure they are clear on what their top three priorities are, and how that relates to the organization's priorities, which will indicate if that strategy is moving forward or not. "The counterintuitive impact of these advances is that they actually make human work truly irreplaceable," Alexander Rinke, the cofounder and CEO of Celonis says. As such, he reminds us, "Humans are much better at processes that involve reasoning, judgment, and interaction with people." So, AI can recommend more accurate and useful opinions to help any managers to solve their managing challenges in office any time.

How AI is eliminating repetitive administrative tasks

There are a lot of tasks that knowledge workers spend time on that provide little—if any—value.For example, say you need to schedule a meeting to get consensus on a decision before moving forward, but you need five people to join the meeting. It's easy to spend a ton of time sending email back-and-forth or finding an open slot on everyone's calendar.That's not the most rewarding use of your time for you or your company.Tools like X.ai give employees AI-powered personal assistants that perform administrative tasks like scheduling, rescheduling, and cancelling meetings.

How AI is transforming internal communications and support

Personnel on the teams that provide employee support have their hands full with other responsibilities, too. HR teams work on building the kind of company people love working for. IT maintains the company's network and keeps data secure. Office managers frequently run big events like holiday parties.These tasks are crucial, but they're often hard for teams to focus on because they're busy answering routine questions. AI service desks like askSpoke allow employee support teams to balance their service commitments with other important responsibilities by reducing interruptions from rote, repetitive requests.Employees can askSpoke for whatever they need over Slack, email, SMS, and the web. askSpoke's friendly AI will automatically provide a prompt response.

How AI is transforming marketing, sales, and customer service AI-powered chatbots help with external support as well. Just like with internal support tools like askSpoke, these chatbots learn from real marketers, salespeople, and customer service reps and are eventually able to answer questions as accurately as a knowledgeable person.For example, chatbot for Messenger helps customers plan their vacations. It books flights, hotels, and cars, highlights destination attractions, and even provides answers to questions like "Where can I go for $100 expense budget only?"

How AI is transforming business data and analytics It's hard to run a competitive business today without data. But even massive amounts of data are useless without a way to transform that data into valuable insights. That's typically why you'd want to hire a data scientist—which just happens to be one of the most difficult roles to fill. How AI is fighting fraud and transforming security. Have you ever taken a call from your bank to find that someone used your debit card fraudulently? Most likely, your bank used some form of AI to detect the fraudulent transaction and decline it. Applying the same basic technology to the workplace helps identify security risks and keeps customer, employee, and company data safe. AI-powered software can automatically detect and address threats among thousands or millions of signals that humans would never be able to parse (especially not in real-time).

How AI is transforming productivity While AI is transforming the workplace in many different ways across every industry, it's impacting productivity most of all. When your office staffs don't have to scroll through calendars to look for open meeting times, build reports in spreadsheets to look for insights, or spend your day answering the same questions over and over again, you're more productive. Workers are freed from redundant and mindless tasks, giving them more time to do work that matters, solve problems, and exercise their creativity. Some tools use AI to specifically monitor and boost productivity. For example, Deloitte's LaborWise provides company leaders and managers with productivity analytics that help them identify areas where labor costs are too high, impediments that slow people down, and departments that need additional staff.

In conclusion, what AI means for the workplace of the future. While some will dramatize the negative impacts of AI, cognitive computing, and robotics, these powerful tools will also help create new jobs, boost productivity, and allow workers to focus on the human aspects of work. Essentially, automation frees companies and their employees up to be more empathetic, to focus on things like the customer experience, employee engagement, and workplace culture.

What are traditional office tools to be replaced by AI ?

Artificial intelligence (AI) is predicted to eliminate over a million jobs in the next few years, potentially replacing lower level positions like administrative assistants with humanoid robots or voice assistants. But in the nearer future, fresh AI-driven software and products are also moving to eliminate non-human elements of the workplace by replacing traditional office tools, including both physical products and everyday electronic processes. Why should businesses switch from the tried-and-true to emerging technology? Many of the experts TechRepublic talked to said the AI options streamline business practices, making their adopters work smarter instead of harder. I shall indicate these office tools ,they can be applied to help any office staffs to finish their these tasks in office, they may include as below:

1. Scheduling

Workloud's end-to-end, cloud-based workforce management software takes scheduling from paper or Excel and moves it to the cloud. Everything from clocking in and out to monitoring employee absences is fully digitalized.Schedules and timesheets are accurate, created easily, and accessible through the service's web, tablet, and mobile apps. The software can also be used for absence management.

2. Employee talent selection

Using AI and organizational behavior science, can be used to replace internal spreadsheets and databases designed to monitor human capital. By mining employee attributes and experiences, the software can recommend who would be best for a project. The software also collects reviews after projects to better predict successful employee-project matches.The traditional hiring process is slow, biased and inaccurate, By removing humans from the beginning stages of the process, it can become faster and more fair, and result in better hires.

AI software automates the hiring process, using online simulations instead of manual screenings and interviews. Using the software, employers can include tasks in a job application, allowing job candidates to show technical skills that may be necessary for a job. Employers can't rule out candidates until they see how the candidate performs, eliminating bias that occurs in the resume reading stage. Both sides also automatically receive updates about each other's steps, reducing the amount of time it takes to .

3.Timesheets: Allocate

Using AI and machine learning, the software registers an employee's computer activity throughout the day. The data, which can also pull information from email and calendars, is used to suggest timesheet entries to reflect a more accurate amount of time an employee spent working. The employee can review and revise as necessary. However, the software doesn't spy on or monitor employees. The data is only available to each employee, while others in the company can only see the timesheet's output, which Allocate said would be the same information available if a manual sheet was used. So,replacing manual timesheets with Allocate has three advantages: More accurate time entry, project analytics, and "'unsucking' the work experience."

4. Document storage

By using AI to read and analyze business and legal documents, AI can store all of the important document-based information in the cloud. The severe reduction in print-outs means less paper and ink, fewer products like binder clips and boxes to store and organize all of the paper, and more employee time freed up from not needing to manually sort through every document.

For example, in any lawyer offices, legal professionals' morale in the industry can suffer when they are pushed into performing such dull, repetitive tasks like sorting through and coding documents by hand, With AI tools to automate those duties, lawyers can focus on more meaningful projects and boost the business's and clients' success as a result. While focused on law firms, businesses that have a lot of unstructured data in documents may also be able to use the service to free up employee time and save on printing costs.

5. Scanners: Adobe Scan

While documents are moving to the cloud more and more, sometimes a physical copy of a document still needs to be scanned using a bulky office scanner. Adobe Scan, an app that condenses a scanner to the size of a smartphone, can rid offices of the need for an in-house scanner. Users can download and open the app, then hold their device over whatever they need to scan. Adobe Sensei then turns the scan into a PDF, and sends it to the Adobe Document Cloud. The app can transform any image into digital text that can then be searched and used electronically. The app streamlines the scanning process, making scans cleaner and more immediate. For businesses already using Adobe services, the app makes documents easily accessible.

6. Landline phones

While landlines in homes are increasingly less common, the same cannot be said for offices. But using chatbots and AI integrations, RingCentral is trying to replace traditional office landline phone systems. The platform offers over 100 integrations, including that AI landline phones can let employees check their voicemail, and a Gong.io option that listens to call recordings to find traits of successful employees than can be used in training. An add-on for Gmail lets users switch from emailing back and forth to a voice session without needing to look up contact information. AI landline phone is easy to adopt and use in the workplace, and is more customizable than standard phone systems, said David Lee, vice president of platform products. Compared to the traditional option, the cloud-based option is "future-proof.

How artificial intelligence can raise office efficiency

Artificial Intelligence is already impacting every industry through automation and machine learning, bringing concerns that AI is on the fast track to replacing many jobs. But these fears aren't new, says Dan Jackson, director of Enterprise Technology at Crestron, a company that designs workplace technology. "I'd argue this is no different than when we moved from an agricultural to an industrial economy at the turn of the last century. The percentage of people working in agriculture significantly decreased, and it was a big shift, but we still have plenty of jobs 100 years later," he says. Anytime society experiences a major technological advancement, we need to be prepared for it to change the way we live and work. It's hard to imagine what the future of jobs will look like with AI, but that future exists. And optimists suggest that, like the sewing machine to the textile industry, AI will make us better, more efficient and faster workers.

In fact, many experts agree that AI has the potential to eliminate mundane, administrative work, while we will always rely on human workers to be empathetic, collaborative, creative and strategic. But it's impact on any industry lies in the hands of the business leaders who are responsible for adopting AI strategies.

● Training presents challenges

A recent study of 1,000 global companies by Accenture found that AI is already creating three new categories of jobs: trainers, explainers and sustainers. Trainers are the people who teach AI systems how to act -- whether it's language, human behavior or the intricacies of human interaction. Explainers are the liaison between technology and business leaders, providing more insight and clarity into machine learning for the non-tech workers. Sustainers are the workers required to maintain AI systems and troubleshoot any potential issues. Some jobs were highly technical and required advanced degrees, but other roles demanded innately human things such as empathy and interaction. Downstream jobs, such as those in sales, marketing, or service will change to take advantage of the insights from AI, but many of the core skills will remain. However, it might sound like any job related to AI will require years of technical knowledge, but that isn't the case. We've already seen a shift in tech hiring -- companies often need highly specific skill sets that are hard to find in potential candidates. As a result, more businesses are hiring employees with the right soft skills, and then training them in technical skills.

An office effort measured approach to AI

The real takeaway is that any approach to AI will need to consider the human aspect of every business. AI has great potential to increase efficiency and accuracy and it's already been proven in certain industries. For example, the use of AI In banking to identify and money laundering schemes. It's also improved healthcare by "increasing the speed and accuracy" of cancer diagnosistics. AI can also help reduce the cost and length of human trafficking investigations, a situation where time is precious. In these examples, AI hasn't replaced jobs, but has positively impacted efficiency.

Thus, we need to ensure our education system responds to equip young people with the appropriate skills and adaptability, while businesses and public organizations must invest in training. Perhaps most of all, we need to encourage imagination and willingness to experiment. The organizations that can innovate with AI will reap the benefits. Their growth will make them the primary source of future jobs. Companies have a choice when implementing AI. They can choose to effectively implement systems that make employee's lives easier and find creative ways to leverage the technology. It's up to employers to ease fears for workers around AI and build strategies that benefit everyone. Hence, some AI experts believe AI can only raise efficiency to some office tasks, however, AI can not still raise efficiency to all office tasks for any office deparments. The reasons are because some office tasks which can only dominate to finish by human office workers. These office tasks are as below:

How can leaders and managers improve employee productivity while still saving time? These below tasks, AI experts ensure that AI can not help any office workers to raise their efficiencies as below:

1. Office managers can not delegate to AI to help them to do. While this tip might seem the most obvious, it is often the most difficult to put into practice. We get it—your company is your baby, so you want to have a direct hand in everything that goes on with it. While there is nothing wrong with prioritizing quality (it is what makes a business successful, after all), checking over every small detail yourself rather than delegating can waste everyone's valuable time. Instead, give responsibilities to qualified employees, and trust that they will perform the tasks well. This gives your employees the opportunity to gain skills and leadership experience that will ultimately benefit your company. You hired them for a reason, now give them a chance to prove you right.

2. Office managers can not match Tasks to Skills to AI. Knowing your employees' skills and behavioral styles is essential for maximizing efficiency. For example, an extroverted, creative, out-of-the-box thinker is probably a great person to pitch ideas to clients. However, they might struggle if they are given a more rule-intensive, detail-oriented task. Asking your employees to be great at everything just isn't efficient—instead, before giving an employee an assignment, ask yourself: is this the person best suited to perform this task? If not, find someone else whose skills and styles match your needs.

3. Office managers can not teach AI to replace them how to communicate and teach their low level staffs how to work effectively. Every manager knows that communication is the key to a productive workforce. Technology has allowed us to contact each other with the mere click of a button (or should we say, tap of a touch screen)—this naturally means that current communication methods are as efficient as possible, right? Not necessarily. A McKinsey study found that emails can take up nearly 28% of an employee's time. In fact, email was revealed to be the second most time-consuming activity for workers (after their job-specific tasks). Instead of relying solely on email, try social networking tools (such as Slack) designed for even quicker team communication. You can also encourage your employees to occasionally adopt a more antiquated form of contact...voice-

to-voice communication. Having a quick meeting or phone call can settle a matter that might have taken hours of back-and-forth emails. All of above communication tasks, I believe that AI can not do better than managers in offices.

4. AI can not keep Goals Clear and focused to be better than managers. You can't expect employees to be efficient if they don't have a focused goal to aim for. If a goal is not clearly defined and actually achievable, employees will be less productive. So, try to make sure employees' assignments are as clear and narrow as possible. Let them know exactly what you expect of them, and tell them specifically what impact this assignment will have. One way to do this is to make sure your goals are "SMART" – specific, measurable, attainable, realistic, and timely. Before assigning an employee a task, ask yourself if it fits each of these requirements. If not, ask yourself how the task can be tweaked to help your workers stay focused and efficient.

5. AI can not know how to incentivize Employees to work more efficiently. One of the best ways to encourage employees to be more efficient is to actually give them a reason to do so. Recognizing your workers for a job well done will make them feel appreciated and encourage them to continue increasing their productivity. When deciding how to reward efficient employees, make sure you take into account their individual needs or preferences. For example, one employee might appreciate public recognition, while another would prefer a private "thank you." In addition to simple words of gratitude, here are a few incentives managers can know how to incentivize their staffs to work efficiently, but AI is only one machine, it can not perform very good.

6. AI does not know how to assist managers to train and Develop employees. Reducing training, or cutting it all together, might seem like a good way to save company time and money (learning on the job is said to be an effective way to train, after all). However, this could ultimately backfire. Forcing employees to learn their jobs on the fly can be extremely inefficient.
So, instead of having workers haphazardly trying to accomplish a task with zero guidance, take the extra day to teach them the necessary skills to do their job. This way, they can set about accomplishing their tasks on their own, and your time won't be wasted down the road answering simple

questions or correcting errors. Past their original training, encourage continued employee development. Helping them expand their skillsets will build a much more advanced workforce, which will benefit your company in the long run. There are a number of ways you can support employee development: individual coaching, workshops, courses, seminars, shadowing or mentoring, or even just increasing their responsibilities. Offering these opportunities will give employees additional skills that allow them to improve their efficiency and productivity. But, AI do not know how to improve any office workers' performance more easily than managers.

● How can AI be dangerous to office working environment?

Most researchers agree that a superintelligent AI is unlikely to exhibit human emotions like love or hate, and that there is no reason to expect AI to become intentionally benevolent or malevolent. Instead, when considering how AI might become a risk to any office working environments, experts think two scenarios most likely:

The AI is programmed to do something devastating: Autonomous weapons are artificial intelligence systems that are programmed to kill. In the hands of the wrong person, these weapons could easily cause mass casualties. Moreover, an AI arms race could inadvertently lead to an AI war that also results in mass casualties. To avoid being thwarted by the enemy, these weapons would be designed to be extremely difficult to simply "turn off," so humans could plausibly lose control of such a situation. This risk is one that's present even with narrow AI, but grows as levels of AI intelligence and autonomy increase. So, if some businessmen apply AI to be business weapon to attack or steal their business competitors' business secret, e.g. contract document, employee performance report, profit report, even business secret document. Then, AI will be one business competitor weapon more than business assistant role in any business market. So, whether AI is office assistant or business competitor weapon, it depends on how the businessmen apply them to assist their business development.

The AI is programmed to do something beneficial, but it develops a destructive method for achieving its goal: This can happen whenever we fail to fully align the AI's goals with ours, which is strikingly difficult. If you ask an obedient intelligent car to take you to the airport as fast as possible, it might get you there chased by helicopters and covered in vomit, doing not what you wanted but literally what you asked for. If a superintelligent system is tasked with a ambitious geoengineering project, it might wreak havoc with our ecosystem as a side effect, and view human attempts to stop it as a threat to be met.

As these examples illustrate, the concern about advanced AI isn't malevolence but competence. A super-intelligent AI will be extremely good at accomplishing its goals, and if those goals aren't aligned with ours, we have a problem. You're probably not an evil ant-hater who steps on ants out of malice, but if you're in charge of a hydroelectric green energy project and there's an anthill in the region to be flooded, too bad for the ants. A key goal of AI safety research is to never place humanity in the position of those ants. Because AI has the potential to become more intelligent than any human, we have no surefire way of predicting how it will behave. We can't use past technological developments as much of a basis because we've never created anything that has the ability to, wittingly or unwittingly, outsmart us. The best example of what we could face may be our own evolution. People now control the planet, not because we're the strongest, fastest or biggest, but because we're the smartest. If we're no longer the smartest, are we assured to remain in control?

A captivating conversation is taking place about the future of artificial intelligence and what it will/should mean for humanity. There are fascinating controversies where the world's leading experts disagree, such as: AI's future impact on the job market; if/when human-level AI will be developed; whether this will lead to an intelligence explosion; and whether this is something we should welcome or fear. But there are also many examples of of boring pseudo-controversies caused by people misunderstanding and talking past each other. To help ourselves focus on the interesting controversies and open questions — and not on the misunderstandings — let's clear up some of the most common myths.

There have been a number of surveys asking AI researchers how many years from now they think we'll have human-level AI with at least 50% probability. All these surveys have the same conclusion: the world's leading experts disagree, so we simply don't know. For example, in such a poll of the AI researchers at the 2015 Puerto Rico AI conference, the average (median) answer was by year 2045, but some researchers guessed hundreds of years or more. There's also a related myth that people who worry about AI think it's only a few years away. In fact, most people on record worrying about superhuman AI guess it's still at least decades away. But they argue that as long as we're not 100% sure that it won't happen this century, it's smart to start safety research now to prepare for the eventuality. Many of the safety problems associated with human-level AI are so hard that they may take decades to solve. So, any businessmen ought have business moralty to know whether they ought how to apply their AI to assist their business development in our future office environment to be more moral.

● Five ways to use AI to improve business efficiency to these office tasks

Regardless of a company's size or type, its executives typically look for ways to help it operate as efficiently as possible. They understand the link between efficiency and profitability. If employees waste too much time with drawn-out processes or complicated tasks, it'll be hard for the enterprise to remain profitable and adapt to challenges. Fortunately, artificial intelligence (AI) supports the need for effective business operations. Here are five ways enterprises can use AI for help: 5 ways to use AI to improve business efficiency image.Getting the best results from AI means looking at where bottlenecks exist, then figuring out if and how it might remove or minimise them. AI can help any offices to improve or raise efficiency to these tasks aspects as below:

1. Use AI to answer queries and support customer engagement

Chatbots are an increasingly popular option for businesses to try, and they use AI to work. Companies often build chatbots that can answer any questions from customers that come through outside of business hours. Some identify the nature of a person's problem, then either attempt to tackle it with preprogrammed answers or pass the communications to a human support worker. The retail industry, in particular, saw success by deploying chatbots. Global data collected by Juniper Research shows an estimated 2.6 billion retail-based chatbot interactions in 2019, and the company forecasts the number to rise to 22 billion in 2023.

Chatbots are excellent for answering simple questions like "How late are you open today?" or "Do you have gluten-free menu options?" Getting quick answers to queries like those increases the chances customers will choose to do business with one company over another. Equally importantly, when chatbots can give responses in a matter of seconds, there's no need for humans to stop what they're doing and address the questions.

2. To enhance reporting speed and accuracy

Company reports reveal things such as which products are selling the fastest and where they're most popular. They can also confirm the impacts of marketing campaigns on product sales, break down the costs of a new packaging choice or shipping method, and much more. However, as anyone that files reports knows, creating them is a painstaking task, and trying to rush through the process could cause mistakes. Some forward-thinking companies are combining AI with big data analytics. Doing this brings better forecasts and takes some of the burdens off the people who prepare the reports. AI also helps conquer the inevitability of mistakes. Even the most careful people make blunders, often because of mental fatigue.

AI learns to spot patterns in data and gets smarter with time. This means reports get finished faster and contain more-reliable information. The reliability aspect is crucial, especially since recently published research indicated two-thirds of the senior executives polled had no confidence or trust in big data. Using AI does not mean companies can do without data scientists. However, depending on the technology allows them to reduce the uncertainty that may otherwise exist. It also prevents employees who work with a company's data from being asked to recheck the findings, even if they initially took appropriate precautions to ensure accuracy.

3. To improve data transfer speeds

Fast data transfers help AI technology work. Concerning some information-intensive applications like virtual reality (VR), any slow transmissions greatly interfere with the realism, and content immersion people should enjoy after strapping on a VR headset. As it turns out, AI can improve data transfer speeds, too. For example, services exist that boost speeds across any wide-area network (WAN). Users enjoy consistently accelerated rates regardless of the kind of information transferred. Some companies have solutions that can reduce WAN job times by up to 98%. These AI-driven options work particularly well when companies need to move information between data centres or cloud environments.

4. To assist the IT team with identifying genuine cyberthreats and anomalies

One of the ongoing challenges faced by IT teams of all sizes is to separate the true cyber threats from false alarms. The difficulties associated with categorising the two types may mean cybersecurity professionals waste time getting to the bottom of things that are ultimately nonissues. They might miss the actual threats that could derail a company's operations. Besides detecting possible intrusions associated with a network, AI can screen for software abnormalities that may make it easier for cybercriminals to orchestrate their attacks successfully. It can also find malicious software hackers installed. Due to this kind of information and the advantages of receiving it through real-time updates, IT security teams can work more productively. They can use the majority of their resources on the threats that matter most to the company's stability.

Some organisations have even used AI to help them conquer the substantial skills shortage in the cybersecurity industry. At Texas A&M University, the Security Operations Center deals with about a million attempted hacks each month. The facility has some full-time workers, but students comprise most of the staff. They work alongside AI that aids in threat monitoring, detection and remediation. Before students see possible threats, the smart technology finds and groups them. This approach saves time and lets the team get to work investigating the problems and deciding how to handle them.

5. To streamline the time-to-hire metric when filling new positions

Statistics show the average time required to hire a person for an open position ranges from 12.7 to 49 days, depending on the industry. The timing also varies based on the type of work a job requires. For example, it takes a shorter amount of time overall to find someone for an administrative or human resources position than one associated with a creative or advertising role. Then, of course, interviews are more extensive for high-profile work.

Human resources professionals increasingly use AI to cut down on the time between first posting a job and finding the ideal individual to hire. For example, an AI platform could look for particular desired keywords in submitted resumes, saving hiring managers from poring over the documents themselves. AI can also pitch in during interviews. A company called VCV recently raised $1.7m to further develop its AI tool that has voice and facial recognition components. Candidates are asked to record videos of them answering interview questions, but they can't prepare for the specific content in advance.

In conclusion, AI Can Boost Efficiency at All Types of Companies. The examples here highlight why so many company leaders conclude that if they use AI, they could cut down on inefficiencies. Getting the best results from AI means looking at where bottlenecks exist, then figuring out if and how it might remove or minimise them. But, AI still lack enough effort to help all staffs to raise efficiency to all department tasks in any office environments.

● How the office energy Department is using AI to solve some of their office staffs electricity toughest challenges in their office working environment.

Insights from artifical intelligence has the potential to transform nearly every aspect of the world as we know it. Today, it is being applied to accelerate the pace of discovery in a wide variety of areas including energy, materials science, health care, national security, emergency response, transportation, and more. AI can be trained to help any energy department to gather data to avoid energy waste to be used to any organizations. So, AI is such as one super machine to do more accurate judgement to help any energy scientists to find the best methods to help any organizations to avoid to waste to use any energy daily. Then, organizations can avoid to spend too much energy to use in offices and they can save more money and avoid energy shortage challenge causes more easily. When the office managers can apply AI ability to reason and put it into a more automated format in a computer system to their every staffs' computer and record their computer electricity use record in their offices every day.

How can AI help offices to save energy or avoid to waste energy ?

The next industrial revolution is already happening. Artificial intelligence (AI) is ushering in an era of technologies that are faster, more adaptable, more efficient, and making the world more digitally connected. AI is best described as complementary to human intelligence, delivering the computing power to crunch numbers too big for people and recognize patterns too tedious for the human eye. In a Harvard Business Review study of 1,500 companies, it was found that the most significant performance improvements were made when humans and machines worked together. As AI becomes one of society's greatest assets, it's especially helpful for solving problems that seem larger than life — like protecting our natural environment.

Through machine learning, robotics, drones, and the internet of things (IoT), society can achieve better monitoring, understanding, and prevention of damage and stressors on Earth's land, air, and water. Even technology already available today could reduce energy usage in the U.S. by 12 to 22 percent, according to The Information Technology Industry Council (ITI). In the face of this dire reality, the potential of technology to help meet this challenge is a rare source of optimism. According to a recent survey by Intel and the research firm Concentrix, 74 percent of business-decision makers working in environmental sustainability agree artificial intelligence (AI) will help solve long-standing environmental challenges; 64 percent agree the Internet of Things (IoT) will help solve these challenges. As the field of AI develops, so will the potential to protect the environment. From the land and air to both drinking and ocean water, AI is shaping up to be the key that governments, organizations, and individuals can tap to work toward a cleaner planet, even AI can help offices to avoid to waste energy when staffs are working in offices every day.

Many AI scientists indicate that AI will also make renewable energy technology like solar panels and wind turbines more efficient and cost effective, helping them to become ubiquitous and lower society's dependence on fossil fuels. AI will also make renewable energy technology like solar panels and wind turbines more efficient and cost effective, helping them to become ubiquitous and lower society's dependence on the fossil fuels polluting the air — then hopefully eliminate them all together. Combined with the smart grid, another technology that will be enabled by AI, this will truly progress the way people receive and use electricity in their homes, offices, and everywhere else. Smart meters save energy by allowing for two-way communication between the grid and anything that uses electricity, giving energy providers a better understanding of usage and the ability to make real-time adjustments for efficiency. Customers will benefit from the real-time data too; seeing the increased costs at peak times will encourage them to voluntarily adjust their usage to save money. This will, in turn, save even more energy: a win-win. Plus, the process of delivering the energy itself will also be improved by the smart grid, thanks to Volt/VAR control systems that can reduce the amount of energy wasted when it's in electricity transmission lines.

Can AI replace office workers

Can AI replace all office workers to do their different tasks in office different department ? If AI can only replace some department office workers to do their simple tasks, how it can raise more efficiency to compare them in some business office environments. I shall indicate some office tasks to explain how AI can help these businesses to raise their efficiency in officesas below:

● AI insurance workers

Nowadays, some country offices begin apply robotics to replace human office workers in their companies. For example, Japanese company replaces office workers with artificial intelligence in insurance industry. A future in which human workers are replaced by machines is about to become a reality at an insurance firm in Japan, where more than 30 employees are being laid off and replaced with an artificial intelligence system that can calculate payouts to policyholders.

Fukoku Mutual Life Insurance believes it will increase productivity by 30% and see a return on its investment in less than two years. The firm said it would save about 140m yen (£1m) a year after the 200m yen (£1.4m)

AI system is installed this month. Maintaining it will cost about 15m yen (£100k) a year. The move is unlikely to be welcomed, however, by 34 employees who will be made redundant by the end of March.

The system is based on IBM's Watson Explorer, which, according to the tech firm, possesses "cognitive technology that can think like a human", enabling it to "analyse and interpret all of your data, including unstructured text, images, audio and video".The technology will be able to read tens of thousands of medical certificates and factor in the length of hospital stays, medical histories and any surgical procedures before calculating payouts, according to the Mainichi Shimbun.

While the use of AI will drastically reduce the time needed to calculate Fukoku Mutual's payouts – which reportedly totalled 132,000 during the current financial year – the sums will not be paid until they have been approved by a member of staff, the newspaper said.

Japan's shrinking, ageing population, coupled with its prowess in robot technology, makes it a prime testing ground for AI. According to a 2015 report by the Nomura Research Institute, nearly half of all jobs in Japan could be performed by robots by 2035. For example, one Japan insurance company, Dai-Ichi Life Insurance has already introduced a Watson-based system to assess payments - although it has not cut staff numbers - and Japan Post Insurance is interested in introducing a similar setup, the Mainichi said. AI could soon be playing a role in the country's politics. Next month, the economy, trade and industry ministry will introduce AI on a trial basis to help civil servants draft answers for ministers during cabinet meetings and parliamentary sessions. The ministry hopes AI will help reduce the punishingly long hours bureaucrats spend preparing written answers for ministers.

● AI public service workers

The automated city: do we still need humans to run public services? If the experiment is a success, it could be adopted by other government agencies, according the Jiji news agency. If, for example a question is asked about energy-saving policies, the AI system will provide civil servants with the relevant data and a list of pertinent debating points based on past answers to similar questions.

The march of Japan's AI robots hasn't been entirely glitch-free, however. At the end of last year a team of researchers abandoned an attempt to develop a robot intelligent enough to pass the entrance exam for the prestigious Tokyo University. "AI is not good at answering the type of questions that require an ability to grasp meanings across a broad spectrum," Noriko Arai, a professor at the National Institute of Informatics, told Kyodo news agency. Hence, AI will have possible to replace some public service workers' tasks.

● AI replace warehouse workers

Denso's use of Drishti shows how some jobs will be transformed by artificial intelligence even when they're unlikely to be eliminated by AI anytime soon. Many jobs in manufacturing require dexterity and resourcefulness, for example, in ways that robots and software still can't match. But advances in AI and sensors are providing new ways to digitize manual labor. That gives managers new insights—and potentially leverage—on workers. For example,some workers say the results are unpleasant. Last year, Amazon warehouse employees in Minnesota staged a walkout to protest how the company uses inventory and worker-tracking technology. They allege that Amazon uses it to enforce a punishing working pace that causes injuries. The company has disputed those claims, saying it coaches employees on how to safely meet quotas.

Workers at Denso were initially wary of the prospect of being video-recorded all day to feed machine-learning algorithms, but Huffman says they have since come to appreciate Drishti's technology. After something goes wrong, workers can now look at the data and video with their managers, instead of having to hope bosses take their account of what happened seriously. Huffman says having a constant readout on productivity also helps managers be more responsive to nascent problems. "If somebody's struggling, not every associate is going to call for help," he says. "If we see their cycle time is jumping through the roof, we can go over and say 'Are you having any issues?'"Workers on Denso lines equipped with Drishti's technology now get a personal feed of their own data. Monitors on each workstation display how a worker is doing, says Raja Shembekar, a Denso vice president. If the worker completes their assembly step on time, they see a smiley face—if not, a frowny one. Hence, Amazon had begun to apply AI robotic to replace some warehouse workers' tasks.

For another factory manufacture working environment example, AI can replace many manufacture workers to do their tasks in factories. Route 9 skims by Boston and cuts clear across Massachusetts to Pittsfield, a city of roughly 50,000, the largest in Berkshire County. Well east of Pittsfield, Route 9 becomes Worcester Road, named for a city that in earlier times was the nation's largest manufacturer of wire—barbed wire, electrical wire, telephone wire and the wire used in the making of undergarments by the

Royal Worcester Corset Co., once the largest employer of women in the United States. Older Worcester residents can still recall the factory bells pealing to signal the start and end of the workday. Now, the bells are silent, and the wire and corset factories have been replaced with three of the nation's largest employers: Walmart, Target and Home Depot. If this sounds familiar, it should. It has been nearly two decades since retail overtook manufacturing as the nation's most important job creator, employing roughly one of every 10 American workers—more people than in health care and construction combined. That's a lot of jobs.

Of course, not all retail jobs qualify as what most of us consider good jobs. Today, the average hourly wage for a nonsupervisory retail worker is $11.24, and less than half of retail workers receive benefits of any kind. Still, as a nation, we've come to a sort of uneasy peace with this trend. We know that manufacturing employs far fewer Americans today than it once did—that iPads and Macs aren't made in America and neither are many televisions, appliances, tools, toys or clothes. We also know that shopping for these appliances, tools, toys and clothes is an all-American pastime: On average, we spend nearly 45 minutes a day (more than 270 hours per year) purchasing goods and services. Retail has become the world as we know it, and many of us expect to make our living working in that world.Thanks to automation and a killer business model, Amazon is so efficient that it reaps nearly twice the revenue per employee of Walmart, despite the fact that Walmart, too, has a substantial online presence. Worldwide, Amazon has installed over 100,000 robots to labor in "perfect symbiosis" with humans in its warehouses and has plans to install many thousands more. While it's not clear what constitutes perfect symbiosis, the robots are said to save the company $22 million annually, per warehouse. The company's master plan of an autonomous future also includes goods delivered by drones and self-driving vehicles.

For while Amazon continues to open warehouses around the globe and staff them with many thousands of human beings, estimates are that every human on the Amazon payroll—whether full- or part-time—displaces two humans at traditional brick-and-mortar operations. And that's a feature, not a bug: As Tim Lindner, a veteran IT analyst, confided in a note to industry insiders, eradicating jobs is the explicit goal of any online retailer. As he once wrote: "Labor is the highest-cost factor in warehouse operations. It is no secret that Amazon is moving to highly automated operations within its distribution centers, and...it has additional technology that can further reduce the number of humans it needs to process customer orders.... You have heard the old programmer's phrase, 'Garbage in, garbage out.'... [With] the diminishing reading abilities of humans on the Receiving dock, finding an automated solution to eliminate the 'garbage in' problem is the holy grail. Amazon may have just patented it."

By garbage, Lindner meant human error, the alternative to which is apparently robotic precision. And robots can be very precise, especially when it comes to routine tasks. Sawyer, an industrial robot created by the former Boston-based Rethink Robotics, offers an impressive illustration of how all-embracing a robot arm can be. Sawyer is the brainchild of Rodney Brooks, the inventor of both Roomba, the robotic vacuum, and PackBot, the robot used to clear bunkers in Iraq and Afghanistan and at the World Trade Center after 9/11. Unlike Roomba and PackBot, Sawyer looks almost human—it has an animated flat-screen face and wheels where its legs should be. Simply grabbing and adjusting its monkey-like arm and guiding it through a series of motions "teaches" Sawyer whatever repeatable procedure one needs it to get done. The robot can sense and manipulate objects almost as quickly and as fluidly as a human and demands very little in return: While traditional industrial robots require costly engineers and programmers to write and debug their code, a high school dropout can learn to program Sawyer in less than five minutes. Brooks once estimated that, all told, Sawyer (and his older brother, the two-armed Baxter robot) would work for a "wage" equivalent of less than $4 an hour.

Robots loom large in discussions of work and its future, a conversation that can get mired in false assumptions. Until recently, many economists were skeptical that automation could permanently displace human workers on a large scale. People have always shifted away from work better done by machines, but the economic principle of "comparative advantage" predicts that humans will maintain an edge in many fields. Under this logic, technology will not displace us but set us free to do less dangerous, more challenging things, essentially the very things that make humans human. Of course, human workers are complicated. We get tired, hungry, distracted, angry, confused. We make mistakes, sometimes egregious ones. Machines lack our frailties and biases and are better equipped to weigh evidence fairly, without prejudice or false assumptions. Perhaps most critically, machines can retain and process data far more accurately than we can, and that data is growing exponentially.

Every minute of every day, Google services 3.6 million searches in the

United States alone. Spammers send 100 million emails. Snapchatters send 527,000 photos, and the Weather Channel broadcasts 18 million forecasts. This and more data—properly collected, codified and analyzed—can be applied to automate almost any high-order task. Data can also serve as a surrogate for human experience and intuition. Online shopping and social media sites "learn" our preferences and use that information to make values-based assessments to influence our decisions and behavior. And, increasingly, machines excel in the tasks once thought uniquely human."Computers are able to see and hear, and have face-recognition capabilities that are significantly better than humans," says Vardi. "Machines understand the human world far better than they did just a few years ago. And we haven't discovered anything in the human brain that can't be modeled."

● AI can replace counter cashier service staffs

And robots need not be perfect, only equal to—or a tad better than—complicated and expensive humans. And technologists are working hard to make sure they are a tad better. For example, in the case of retail, it's become clear that many of us avoid the self-service checkout line—we prefer the cashier to punch in our purchases rather than do so ourselves. So it seems that the job of cashier—among the largest retail employment categories—is not directly at risk. But Zeynep Ton, an MIT management expert who focuses on the retail sector, says self-service checkout is only a first step and not a terribly smart one. "Customers recognized that self-service checkout is not an innovation, but merely a way of outsourcing the job to them, so they didn't like it," she says. "But new technology is coming that will make self-service checkout so much easier and faster, and that will have a real impact on retail employment."

Experts caution that the so-called apocalypse in retail predicted a few years ago has not yet come to pass. In fact, for every company closing existing stores, two more are opening new stores. Retail is a highly competitive industry, and technology is transforming not only the way we shop but the way we connect with brands—for example, just a few years ago, who would have imagined that Amazon would open actual retail stores? And while e-commerce has grown to 10 percent of retail, that still leaves 90 percent for brick-and-mortar stores. But those brick-and-mortar stores, too, are undergoing radical change that has serious implications for America's workforce.

As example, Lobaugh cites food trucks, which he says increasingly pose a threat to many fast-food outlets. Unlike restaurants pinned down by a pair of Golden Arches, food trucks are nimble—they can home in on areas where customers are most likely to gather at any particular time. They can also tailor their offerings to a particular region or even a neighborhood, as well as use Facebook or other media to get out the word on their menu items and locations. Small, specialty stores also have far more flexibility than large department stores. "Technology has reduced the cost of entry into new markets, so in retail there are fewer big, monolithic companies, but more small competitors," he says. "Companies are diversifying to meet the specific needs and desires of consumers—everyone's piece is getting smaller, but there are many more pieces."

But despite what it predicts will be a banner holiday season, this year Amazon took on far fewer seasonal employees than usual—100,000 employees versus 120,000 the previous two years. And while an Amazon spokeswoman insisted that automation is not a factor in this reduced workforce, others seem to not agree. In a recent report, Morgan Stanley analyst Brian Nowak soothed the fears of Amazon shareholders concerned with the wage increase by pointing out that automation had already and would continue to reduce the call for labor, and therefore reduce overall costs. When asked about this, Lobaugh again tactfully declined to comment—other than to say that while the retail sector had lost less ground than most people assume, retail employees were another matter. "There are winners," he says, "and then there are losers."

● AI can replace accountants in accountancy service industry

Not that long ago artificial intelligence (AI), robots and machine learning (ML) were thought to be things only found in science fiction films. Today, this type of technology is taking center stage in workplaces across the globe. Industries, including manufacturing, retail, agriculture, and customer service have already had AI replace some job positions that left workers scrambling to find new career options. This AI revolution is not expected to slow down anytime soon. In fact, experts anticipate that as many as 800 million jobs could be replaced with AI technology by the year 2030. Initially, AI technology and automation in the workplace seemed to only affect pink and blue-collar workers. As this technology advances and becomes more powerful, professional, white-collar workers, including accountants, are starting to worry about what the future holds for their career and if AI will be developed to own their professional skills in accounting service industry.

In basic terms, AI technology is intelligent machines that are able to complete repetitive, mundane tasks at a fraction of the time it takes humans and with greater accuracy. The emergence of Machine Learning now allows AI platforms to observe, analyze and self-learn data and processes to improve its performance and accuracy over time. AI technology is already able to handle many accounting functions, such as tax preparation, payroll, and audits. Many of the leading accounting software providers, including Xero, Intuit and Sage have incorporated AI technology into their software to handle basic accounting tasks, such as bank reconciliations, invoice categorization, risk assessment, and audit processes, like expense submissions and invoice payments. Many of these standard tasks are extremely time-consuming, which has many accountants across the country worried about how the emerging AI technology will affect their billable hours. An even bigger concern is that AI technologies will replace the need for companies to work with accountants at all.

● AI Will Transform not Replace Accountants

While there is no doubt that AI technology is capable of handling many standard accounting tasks faster and more efficiently or that these capabilities will only increase over time, it doesn't mean the end for accountants. There always will be a need for that human element - human intelligence - at the other end of AI technology. In fact, according to leading research firm, Gartner, AI is set to create more jobs than it will replace, leaving workers, including accountants with options. Accountants don't have to worry about their job being replaced by AI any time in the near future. Companies will always need accountants that can analyze and interpret AI data, as well as provide consulting services. Rather than replacing the role of an accountant, AI technology will transform the duties an accountant performs.

With AI technology and machine learning handling many of the mundane, repetitive tasks, accountants will have more time to focus on other aspects of the job, such as consulting and data analysis. This is good news for many accountants. Rather than spending hours completing menial tasks, accountants of the future will be able to use and analyze AI data to provide their clients with sound business solutions.

In many ways, AI will help accountants improve their services. AI technology will improve data entry accuracy and lower the liability risk for accountants. In addition, emerging technology is more efficient at fraud detection, adding an extra layer of protection for accountants and their clients. It also provides real-time data, which allows accountants to provide real-time solutions. Even more impressive is the ability of machine learning to analyze large amounts of data instantly, evaluate past successes and failures in an effort to accurately predict future outcomes.

There is no way to escape the use of AI technology, at least not if you hope to remain competitive in the upcoming years. The speed, efficiency and accuracy of AI technology just cannot be beat. The only thing accountants can do is to embrace this new technology and learn how to maximize its use. The better equipped you are to help your clients integrate and utilize AI technology in their accounting processes the more valuable you will be. For example, many universities today are already incorporating IT and database management courses into their accounting program. This means that graduating students are coming into the workforce with the skills they need for future accounting work. Accountants already in the workforce must find ways to acquire these skills in order to remain relevant to their employers and/or their clients. Accountants can obtain the IT skills they need by attending seminars, using self-learning online programs or attending college-level courses. It is equally important for accountants to stay up-to-date on the latest accounting trends, emerging technologies and industry news. This will allows accountants to not only keep their jobs but to also provide more efficient services to their clients. Rather than worry about AI taking over their jobs, accountants should embrace this technology as a powerful solution to enhance customer services. Finally, accountants will be able to use all their training and experience to provide customer will real and effective business solutions, whether it's in reference to tax consulting, real estate deals, mergers, growth options, or any other business practice.

On conclusion, technology is advancing at record rates so now is the time to obtain the IT and database management skills you need to advance into the future. With the right skills and training, accountants are guaranteed a lucrative career that will last well into the future.

Why Developed And Developing Countries Need Artificial Intelligent Development To Assist Office Tasks

Must developed and developing countries need artificial intelligent development to assist office tasks ? Ought AI is needed to prefer to develop technique to assist office staffs to reduce workload to compare other kinds of occupation environment tasks aspects ? If one developed country, e.g. US, UK , Japan , Singapore it does not continue to develop artificial intelligence, robotic, then what disadvantges or weaknesses , it will encounter to compare when it chooses to continue to develop this artificial intelligent technology in society. If one developing country, e.g. China, Korea, Taiwan, it does not continue to develop artificial intelligence, robotic, then what disadantages or weaknesses, it will also encounter to compare when it chooses to continue to develop this artificial intelligent technology in in society. I shall explan the reasons why the results may cause to either the developed country, or the developing country as below:

● How AI help developing countries to communication and agriculture and learning and medical delivery development

Why can AI help developing countries ? Drones that pick inaccessible crops and mobile phones that give medical advice are two of the ways AI can transform life in the developing world. Artificial intelligence (AI) may improve the lives of the world's poor, the technology needed to revolutionise inefficient, ineffective food and healthcare systems in developing countries is well. For example, in low-income areas, agriculture and healthcare are two critical ecosystems that we can apply AI to immediately; this is not the far future, or even in five years.

Artificial intelligence (AI) has seeped into the daily lives of people in the developed world. From virtual assistants to recommendation engines, AI is in the news, our homes and offices. There is a lot of potential in terms of AI usage, especially in humanitarian areas. The impact could have a multiplier effect in developing countries, where resources are limited.

Emergency Response to developing countries' earthquake natural damage suddence occurrence predicting

AI and machine learning are still finding importance in emerging markets, but certain applications have emerged and are now widely used. For instance, predictive models for disaster relief enable first responders to automatically analyze large-scale behavior and movement through multiple sources of data including social media platforms, web forums, news sources, etc. Based on collected data, responders can scale reconstruction efforts and distribute supplies in a timely manner.

Why and how AI can assist farmers to predict when the earthquake occurs suddenly in order to avoid or reduce the natural damage to their agriculture productive number loss. For example, In 2015, when a major earthquake hit Nepal, more than 8 million people were affected. During the aftermath, drones were used to map and assess the destruction and speed up the rescue mission. The town of Sankhu, situated about 20 kilometers northeast of

Kathmandu, was among the highly affected locations. In May 2018, my company Fusemachines and GeoSpatial Systems partnered with Sankhu's city officials to use drones and artificial intelligence in an effort to automatically estimate the reconstruction need. After processing data accumulated from a drone-powered aerial mapping of the region, the team fed this data to advanced machine learning algorithms. Combining drone imagery, digital mapping and machine learning, the team configured region modeling and infrastructure development with higher accuracy. Another organization known as One Concern, a California-based startup, has created a predictive AI program called Seismic Concern to accurately predict seism and is also working on solutions for wildfires, floods and hurricanes.

Smart AI Agriculture

Another application of AI in developing countries is smart agriculture. Farmers monitor crops more effectively and make better predictions on planting, weeding and harvesting using AI tools. It can also be used to analyze one plant at a time and add pesticides only to infected plants and trees instead of spraying pesticides across large swaths of crops. One California-based tech company is an example of this use of AI. So, the developing countries farmers in rural parts of India are also using AI to increase yields through better access to information about the farming season than they would normally have. Technology-enabled process automation offers the agribusiness industry the chance for remarkable growth -- not only in developed countries but around the world. There's a unique opportunity to increase yields, cut down labor costs and improve people's health.

Medicine Delivery to developing countries' patients urgent need

Companies are also leveraging AI to improve access to health care in some of the most remote areas of the world. In Rwanda, for example, Zipline is using drones to deliver medical supplies and blood to hospitals and clinics that are difficult to access by car. This has dramatically impacted people living in remote parts of the country because they are able to get medical help when needed. The drone system in Rwanda has also helped reduce waste of blood by 95%, as noted by Zipline. One Concern has created an AI program called Seismic Concern that accurately predicts seismic events and is also working on solutions for floods, wildfires and hurricanes. The medical field may actually benefit the most from emerging technologies in developing countries.

Assistance to reduce teaching work workload or psychological pressure to teachers in developing countries' schools

Another vital area benefiting from innovative technologies like AI is education. Advanced technologies can enhance how we learn, teach and perform tasks. In most developing countries, schools lack experienced teachers and resources to enhance students' knowledge. As a result, many students still have to walk long distances to get to the nearest school, which has created education gaps, especially in rural areas. AI tools such as personalized learning assistants can simplify learning by making tutoring services and learning materials accessible to all students, wherever they are. Machines can be automated to help students learn basic concepts without a tutor, which companies like Carnegie Learning are working on. This would allow students to learn at any time from anywhere. With AI, education is made easy and accessible to more people.

The initial usage of AI in developing countries has been at a micro level -- solving small, specific problems in a defined industry. As machine learning advances and there is a higher utilization of AI, we will see more complex issues being targeted and resolved. When duly adopted, AI can positively impact future developing countries people everyday lives not just in disaster intervention, education, health care and agriculture but can also help in mitigating poverty, malnutrition and pollution. Especially, in developing nations, to leverage AI's true potential and create a snowball effect. Startups are defining a holistic and humanitarian approach to building more sophisticated, AI-ready societies. Stakeholders in the AI landscape should understand the strengths and nuances of the developing world as well as the limitations of AI and create localized solutions and applications.

Why does smart phone help developing countries communication ?

Internet Seen as Positive Influence on Education but Negative on Morality in Emerging and Developing Nations. Internet access differs substantially across the 32 emerging and developing countries polled, with the lowest rates of internet use in South Asian and sub-Saharan African nations. Within countries, computer owners, young people, the well-educated, the wealthy and those with English language ability are much more likely to access the internet than their counterparts. To access the internet, people increasingly use smartphones rather than more cumbersome fixed landline connections and computers. Around the world, both smartphones and basic-feature phones alike are used for sending messages and taking pictures.

In fact, many developing countries young people, students are popular to use smart phones for internet usage aim, instead of communication. Moreover, many developing countries working people are also popular to use smart phones for any working usage in their working time , even non working time any time. So, smart phones (AI) phones will be important communication or leisure tools to developing countries people in the future. Unless, it is one day, scientists can develop another new communication tool to replace smart phones. So, artificial intelligence will be important to influence developing countries people , how to improve or bring positive learning attitudes to students in their daily learnnng lifes. as well as how to raise developing countries people, how to raise working people efficiency or improve performace in their daily working lifes. So, AI may bring positive learning or working attitudes to developing countries working people and students both.

The Positive Impact of Mass Media in Developing Countries

Radio, newspapers, television, Internet, social media, etc., all of these are forms of mass media. Each of these outlets has the capability of bringing information to thousands of people with one device. While in some communities it is easy to take advantage of these communication outlets such as television and Internet access, not everyone has access to such outlets. Radio is one of the most common forms of mass media in developing countries because it's affordable and uses less electricity than many other forms of mass media, but only approximately 75 percent of people in developing countries have access to a radio, and roughly 77 percent of people in rural areas have access to electricity.

For developing countries that have implemented forms of mass media in their communities, there have been numerous positive outcomes are influenced to impact developing countries mass media by artificial intelligence as below:

When AI is participated to developing countries mass media, it can influence any radio, television audiences raise more attention to each other through social media platforms such as Facebook and Twitter and create, organize and initiate street protests and campaigns. Furthermore, having access to social media in developing countries, people are able to connect to those that they usually wouldn't have the chance to talk to. Moreover, AI Provides educational opportunities- In many countries, the division between local and national languages as well as issues of literacy can make communication difficult. With the use of mass media, a bridge can be built between these two gaps. In India, there is a radio station that provides information in local languages and respects local culture and traditions. One of the main ways is to create public awareness of what is going on with businesses and government officials. The media plays an important role in giving people the opportunity to act against injustice, oppression and misdeeds that they otherwise wouldn't know about. Information on available healthcare, a mass radio broadcast was sent out encouraging parents to seek treatment at local healthcare facilities for their sick children. With this mass outreach on healthcare, the encouragement of people to take their children to healthcare facilities saved thousands of lives. This easy way of encouraging others and bringing awareness about certain diseases was made possible through a simple radio broadcast. Finally, when AI is particiapted to media, it may bring many social issues to life that otherwise would remain unknown to many people. In developing countries and communities like Burkina Faso, when the radio broadcast was released about malaria, diarrhea and pneumonia, people were educated and moved to action and knew to take their children to healthcare facilities for preventative care. As it is seen, having access to different media outlets is vital for those in developing countries. Here are three ways that those in developing countries can implement mass media to help their people and communities.

When AI is participated to any internet radio or internet newspaper mass online listening or reading channel. It can provide online radios or newspapers in public places- By providing online radios and newspapers in public areas it gives community members to access news, information and emergency warnings. Even though radios can be on the cheaper side, there are still many people that can't afford to have a radio in their home. By providing one in a local place, not only would it better educate the community members but also it will bring the community together. So, it can make media outlets a two-way platform- Creating a two-way platform between the community and those who are behind the radio stations, newspapers or broadcasts makes the community feel involved and that their voices are being heard. An organization called Soul City in sub-Saharan Africa is showing how well two-way platforms work by engaging their listeners and having them contribute thoughts and ideas about complex issues. Because developing countries radio listening audiences or newspaper readers are popular to accept computer online radio listening channel or online newspaper reading channel to replace traditional paper newspapers or radio machines. So, AI may raise their listening news or reading news leisure feeling from online mass media channel in the future.

● Why do developed countries need to develop AI
Artificial intelligence, or AI, is driving massive shifts across the globe, and every day more questions arise. What impact will AI have on the workforce and how can we prepare for it? How can we encourage economy-boosting and job-creating technologies? How can we ensure that AI will be implemented ethically and with minimal bias? How will society benefit? For developed country, such as US example. None of the US, Israel and Russia have a formal national AI policy yet. Private sector companies such as Google, Amazon and Apple and the US department of defence are driving the bulk of AI investment in the United States. Though Israel does not have a specific policy, it is keenly focused on AI and has seen the number of AI start-ups triple since 2014.

Developed country may learn whether what weakness it is lacking when it does not continue to develop AI from one another developed country. Which countries are approaching AI most effectively, and to what degree is there opportunity for greater international collaboration? It may be too early to tell; however, when analyzing the best practices of existing national AI policies, there is much that can be learned. These are the specific areas to consider. When one developed country continue to develop or research AI, it may bring these benefits as below:

On gathering Data aspect, from self-driving vehicles to smart cities, data is the driver behind AI. Innovation in the United States is limited without a national strategy that answers questions about protocol and ownership. France and Denmark, on the other hand, are opening government data. France is hosting troves of centrally collected public and private data that it plans to make available as part of its strategy. Conversely, by taking a restrictive position on issues of data collection (as indicated by the implementation of General Data Protection Regulation), the EU is putting manufacturers and software designers at a disadvantage while balancing the demand for privacy. On raising technologica talent aspect, the demand for AI talent far outweighs the available supply. As a result, almost every nation's strategy addresses talent development. Canada's AI strategy is distinct in that it primarily focuses on research and talent strategy. The country boasts AI degree programmes and is building a $127 million research facility in Toronto. Companies like Facebook and my own company, Uptake, are investing in Canada to access this talent pool. On AI legal technological innovation aspect, a whole host of legal questions swirl around AI. The country is developing a bill for AI liability that will be ready in March 2019. The government hopes the legal framework will attract investors by providing a simple, comprehensive guideline to enable the broad use of AI systems. So, when the developed country applied AI technology to assist any lawyers to work, then AI can help them to reduce the workload to draft any legal documents more easier. So, any developed countries lawyers' draft legal documents time must reduce if the developed countries lawyers accept to apply AI to assist their legal works. One of the great promises of AI is its potential for improving quality of life. But without the right planning and oversight, we risk exacerbating problems of inequality or marginalizing groups of people. As an example, India's AI strategy is focused on leveraging the technology not only for economic growth, but also for social inclusion.

AI may bring what benefits to developed countries
From SIRI to self-driving cars, artificial intelligence (AI) is progressing rapidly. While science fiction often portrays AI as robots with human-like characteristics, AI can encompass anything from Google's search algorithms to IBM's Watson to autonomous weapons. Artificial intelligence today is properly known as narrow AI (or weak AI), in that it is designed to perform a narrow task (e.g. only facial recognition or only internet searches or only driving a car). However, the long-term goal of many researchers is to create general AI (AGI or strong AI). While narrow AI may outperform humans at whatever its specific task is, like playing chess or solving equations, AGI would outperform humans at nearly every cognitive task.

Why research AI safety? Would AI bring war when AI is continued to develop by developed countries? In the near term, the goal of keeping AI's impact on society beneficial motivates research in many areas, from economics and law to technical topics such as verification, validity, security and control. Whereas it may be little more than a minor nuisance if your laptop crashes or gets hacked, it becomes all the more important that an AI system does what you want it to do if it controls your car, your airplane, your pacemaker, your automated trading system or your power grid. Another short-term challenge is preventing a devastating arms race in lethal autonomous weapons.

In the long term, an important question is what will happen if the quest for strong AI succeeds and an AI system becomes better than humans at all cognitive tasks. As pointed out by I.J. Good in 1965, designing smarter AI systems is itself a cognitive task. Such a system could potentially undergo recursive self-improvement, triggering an intelligence explosion leaving human intellect far behind. By inventing revolutionary new technologies, such a superintelligence might help us eradicate war, disease, and poverty, and so the creation of strong AI might be the biggest event in human history. Some experts have expressed concern, though, that it might also be the last, unless we learn to align the goals of the AI with ours before it becomes superintelligent.

There are some who question whether strong AI will ever be achieved, and others who insist that the creation of superintelligent AI is guaranteed to be beneficial. At FLI we recognize both of these possibilities, but also recognize the potential for an artificial intelligence system to intentionally or unintentionally cause great harm. We believe research today will help us better prepare for and prevent such potentially negative consequences in the future, thus enjoying the benefits of AI while avoiding pitfalls.

How can AI be dangerous when developed countries continue to develop AI to become weapon to replace soldiers?

Most researchers agree that a superintelligent AI is unlikely to exhibit human emotions like love or hate, and that there is no reason to expect AI to become intentionally benevolent or malevolent. Instead, when considering how AI might become a risk, experts think two scenarios most likely:

The AI is programmed to do something devastating: Autonomous weapons are artificial intelligence systems that are programmed to kill. In the hands of the wrong person, these weapons could easily cause mass casualties. Moreover, an AI arms race could inadvertently lead to an AI war that also results in mass casualties. To avoid being thwarted by the enemy, these weapons would be designed to be extremely difficult to simply "turn off," so humans could plausibly lose control of such a situation. This risk is one that's present even with narrow AI, but grows as levels of AI intelligence and autonomy increase.

The AI is programmed to do something beneficial, but it develops a destructive method for achieving its goal: This can happen whenever we fail to fully align the AI's goals with ours, which is strikingly difficult. If you ask an obedient intelligent car to take you to the airport as fast as possible, it might get you there chased by helicopters and covered in vomit, doing not what you wanted but literally what you asked for. If a superintelligent system is tasked with a ambitious geoengineering project, it might wreak havoc with our ecosystem as a side effect, and view human attempts to stop it as a threat to be met. So, a super-intelligent AI will be extremely good at accomplishing its goals, and if those goals aren't aligned with ours, we have a problem. You're probably not an evil ant-hater who steps on ants out of malice, but if you're in charge of a hydroelectric green energy project and there's an anthill in the region to be flooded, too bad for the ants. A key goal of AI safety research is to never place humanity in the position of those ants.

Why the recent interest in AI safety ?

Stephen Hawking, Elon Musk, Steve Wozniak, Bill Gates, and many other big names in science and technology have recently expressed concern in the media and via open letters about the risks posed by AI, joined by many leading AI researchers. The idea that the quest for strong AI would ultimately succeed was long thought of as science fiction, centuries or more away. However, thanks to recent breakthroughs, many AI milestones, which experts viewed as decades away merely five years ago, have now been reached, making many experts take seriously the possibility of superintelligence in our lifetime. While some experts still guess that human-level AI is centuries away, most AI researches at the 2015 Puerto Rico Conference guessed that it would happen before 2060. Since it may take decades to complete the required safety research, it is prudent to start it now.

Because AI has the potential to become more intelligent than any human, we have no surprise way of predicting how it will behave. We can't use past technological developments as much of a basis because we've never created anything that has the ability to, wittingly or unwittingly, outsmart us. The best example of what we could face may be our own evolution. People now control the planet, not because we're the strongest, fastest or biggest, but because we're the smartest. If we're no longer the smartest, are we assured to remain in control?

A captivating conversation is taking place about the future of artificial intelligence and what it will/should mean for humanity. There are fascinating controversies where the world's leading experts disagree, such as: AI's future impact on the job market; if/when human-level AI will be developed; whether this will lead to an intelligence explosion; and whether this is something we should welcome or fear. But there are also many examples of of boring pseudo-controversies caused by people misunderstanding and talking past each other. When one developed country continue to develop AI, can itself country's all factories workers will lose jobs, due to AI can replace them to do simple works in factories, or any public transport drivers, e.g. bus drivers, ferry , tram, train drivers, they will lose jobs, when AI (non manual driving drivers) can replace all public transport drivers. So, some occupations will lose if developed countries continue to develop or research AI to replace human to do some simple jobs, such as some cooking jobs can be done by AI. So, it is possible that future cookers won't be needed, because AI cooking skills may be better than them to cook any good taste chinese or western food in restaurants. If you drive down the road, you have a subjective experience of colors, sounds, etc. But does a self-driving car have a subjective experience? Does it feel like anything at all to be a self-driving car? Although this mystery of consciousness is interesting in its own right, it's irrelevant to AI risk. If you get struck by a driverless car, it makes no difference to you whether it subjectively feels conscious. In the same way, what will affect us humans is what superintelligent AI does, not how it subjectively feels.

In fact, AI may be make any brokers jobs in financial market. the main concern of the beneficial-AI movement isn't with robots but with intelligence itself: specifically, intelligence whose goals are misaligned with ours. To cause us trouble, such misaligned superhuman intelligence needs no robotic body, merely an internet connection – this may enable outsmarting financial markets, out-inventing human researchers, out-manipulating human leaders, and developing weapons we cannot even understand. Even if building robots were physically impossible, a super-intelligent and super-wealthy AI could easily pay or manipulate many humans to unwittingly do its bidding. So, future brokers will be replaced by AI, when AI can be made to own financial brokers' analytical mind to make more accurate whether the share price will rise up or fall down to compare human financial brokers' analytical mind. The robot misconception is related to the myth that machines can't control humans. Intelligence enables control: humans control tigers not because we are stronger, but because we are smarter. This means that if we cede our position as smartest on our planet, it's possible that we might also cede control.

Not wasting time on the above-mentioned misconceptions lets us focus on true and interesting controversies where even the experts disagree. What sort of future do you want? Should we develop lethal autonomous weapons? What would you like to happen with job automation? What career advice would you give today's kids? Do you prefer new jobs replacing the old ones, or a jobless society where everyone enjoys a life of leisure and machine-produced wealth? Further down the road, would you like us to create superintelligent life and spread it through our cosmos? Will we control intelligent machines or will they control us? Will intelligent machines replace us, coexist with us, or merge with us? What will it mean to be human in the age of artificial intelligence?

Why do developed countries people need AI ?

Why do we assume that AI will require more and more physical space and more power when human intelligence continuously manages to miniaturize and reduce power consumption of its devices. How low the power needs and how small will the machines be by the time quantum computing becomes reality? Why do we assume that AI will exist as independent machines? If so, and the AI is able to improve its Intelligence by reprogramming itself, will machines driven by slower processors feel threatened, not by mere stupid humans, but by machines with faster processors? What would drive machines to reproduce themselves when there is no biological incentive, pressure or need to do so?

Who says superior AI will need or want to have a physical existence when an immaterial AI could evolve and preserve itself better from external dangers. What will happen if AI developed by competing ideologies, liberalism vs communism, reach maturity at the same time, will they fight for hegemony by trying to destroy each other physically and/or virtually. If AI is programmed to believe in God, and competing AI emerges programmed by muslims, christians or jews, how are the different AI's going to make sense of the different religious beliefs, are we going to have AI religious wars? What if the "powers that be" greatest fear is the emergence of a super AI that police's and rationalizes the distribution of wealth and food. A friendly super AI that is programmed to help humanity by, enforcing the declaration of Human Rights (the US is the only industrialized country that to this day has not signed this declaration) ending corruption and racism and protecting the environment.Most benefits of civilization stem from intelligence, so how can we enhance these benefits with artificial intelligence without being replaced on the job market and perhaps altogether?

Key to the process of machine learning are neural networks. These are brain-inspired networks of interconnected layers of algorithms, called neurons, that feed data into each other, and which can be trained to carry out specific tasks by modifying the importance attributed to input data as it passes between the layers. During training of these neural networks, the weights attached to different inputs will continue to be varied until the output from the neural network is very close to what is desired, at which point the network will have 'learned' how to carry out a particular task. A subset of machine learning is deep learning, where neural networks are expanded into sprawling networks with a huge number of layers that are trained using massive amounts of data. It is these deep neural networks that have fuelled the current leap forward in the ability of computers to carry out task like speech recognition and computer vision.

In conclusion, when developed countries continue to develop AI, it may bring positive advantages to bring raising productivies, or efficiencies, but it may also raise unemployment ratio to any low skill or low knowledge jobs in ther societies. However, human future society will need to change to be better to raise our living standard. But AI is one kind the best choice tool to achieve this aim in our future, so I agree developed countries continue to develop or research AI to be the super -human machine.

Artificial Intelligence Worker Brings

Working Environment Influences

Robots were once known only for the manufacturing business but today they are very much part of many workplaces. The future is even more promising for this wonder of artificial intelligence.Imagine a robot doing some of the major tasks of managers like using data to evaluate problems, making better decisions, monitoring team performance, and even setting goals.

Technology is playing a pivotal role in helping humans work more effectively. Since automation has become an integral part of business operations, we can predict that robots are soon going to replace many jobs that are today performed by humans. Now that the corporate world is also on the cusp of entering the robotic age, let's see what pros and cons this technology offers business world. If one day, our global working environments have any kinds of robotic participates to our service and warehouse and office etc. different working environment in order to assist office workers, service workers, warehouse workers, professional lawyers, doctors accountants job duties, what positive or negative influences, it will bring to what negative or positive effects to any office , warehouse, shopping centre, hospital, transport , restaurant etc, different working environments. Can robotic help office , warehouse to raise efficency ? Can robotic help hospital, restaurant, cinema, shopping center to improve service performance? Can robotic influence working environment to be worse? Can robotic help office or any working places to reduce expenditure or reduce long time machine and salary cost when they do not need more employees or machines , due to robotic workers assistance.

I shall attempt to explain whether robotic workers will bring what positive or negative influence to our future working environment as below:

Advantages to robotic bring to working environment

What advantages thar robotic will bring to working environment? They may include: Many people fear that robots or full automation may someday take their jobs, but this is simply not the case. Robots bring more advantages than disadvantages to the workplace. They enrich a company's ability to succeed while improving the lives of real, human employees who are still needed to keep operations running smoothly. If you're thinking about investing in some robots, share the advantages with your employees. You might be surprised at how many of them are quick to support the idea.

1. Safety

Safety is the most obvious advantage of utilizing robotics. Heavy machinery, machinery that runs at hot temperature, and sharp objects can easily injure a human being. By delegating dangerous tasks to a robot, you're more likely to look at a repair bill than a serious medical bill or a lawsuit. Employees who work dangerous jobs will be thankful that robots can remove some of the risks.

2. Speed

Robots don't get distracted or need to take breaks. They don't request vacation time or ask to leave an hour early. A robot will never feel stressed out and start running slower. They also don't need to be invited to employee meetings or training session. Robots can work all the time, and this speeds up production. They keep your employees from having to overwork themselves to meet high pressure deadlines or seemingly impossible standards.

3. Consistency

Robots never need to divide their attention between a multitude of things. Their work is never contingent on the work of other people. They won't have unexpected emergencies, and they won't need to be relocated to complete a different time sensitive task. They're always there, and they're doing what they're supposed to do. Automation is typically far more reliable than human labor.

4. Perfection

Robots will always deliver quality. Since they're programmed for precise, repetitive motion, they're less likely to make mistakes. In some ways, robots are simultaneously an employee and a quality control system. A lack of quirks and preferences, combined with the eliminated possibility of human error, will create a predictably perfect product every time.

5. Happier Employees

Since robots are often assigned to perform tasks that people don't particularly enjoy, like menial work, repetitive motion, or dangerous jobs, your employees are more likely to be happy. They'll be focusing on more engaging work that's less likely to grind down their nerves. They might want to take advantage of additional educational opportunities, utilize your employee wellness program, or participate in an innovative workplace project. They'll be happy to let the robots do the work that leaves them feeling burned out.

6. Job Creation

Robots don't take jobs away. They merely change the jobs that exist. Robots need people for monitoring and supervision. The more robots we need, the more people we'll need to build those robots. By training your employees to work with robots, you're giving them a reason to stay motivated in their position with your company. They'll be there for the advancements and they'll have the unique opportunity to develop a new set of tech or engineering related skills.

7. Productivity

Robots can't do everything. Some jobs absolutely need to be completed by a human. If your human employees aren't caught up doing the things that could have easily be left for robots, they'll be available and productive. They can talk to customers, answer emails and social media comments, help with branding and marketing, and sell products. You'll be amazed at how much they can accomplish when the grunt work isn't weighing them down.

8. Cost reduce

The first and the foremost advantage of having robots in workplaces is their cost. Robots are much cheaper than humans and their cost is now decreasing. It's a fact that we cannot compare human abilities with robots but robotic capabilities are now growing quickly. For example, if you run an essay writing service, you can use robots to perform every kind of research related to any subject. Because robots are more active and don't get tired like humans, the collaboration between humans and robots is reducing absenteeism. The pace of human cannot increase hence robots are helping humans.

However,robots are more precise than humans; they don't tremble or shake as human hands. Robots have smaller and versatile moving parts which help them in performing tasks with more accuracy than humans. There is no doubt that robots are significantly stronger and faster than humans. Robots come in any shape and size, depending upon the need of the task. Robots can work anywhere in any environmental condition whether it is space, underwater, in extreme heat or wind etc. Robots can be used everywhere where human safety is a huge concern. Robots are programmed by a human; they cannot say no to anything and can be used for any dangerous and unwanted work where humans may deny to offer their services. For example, many robotic probes have been sent into space but have never returned. Robots in warfare are saving more lives and have now proven to be very successful. For example, in chemical factory environment, robots are now being used in the chemical industry and can, for example deal with chemical spills in a nuclear plant, which would otherwise pose a major health concern. Cost-effectiveness is one of the most sound arguments to be made for the case of industrial robots. Robots will reduce production costs by eliminating internal costs to compensate human salaries. Businesses are forecasting that their profitability will increase once they implement robots into production, or that they will have more financial mobility to invest in new products or technologies.

9. productive efficiency

Quality assurance is expected with the use of machinery in production. Industrial robots will be able to ensure consistency with mass production of manufactured products. The possible human error that assembly line workers pose the threat of will be removed. Optimized production efficiency means that a general manager will be able to have set quantity and quality standards that will be met by robots. Production quotas will not be jeopardized by low concentration, break time and employee injuries, among other things. The efficiency of production forecasts and supply levels will be increased with robots, able to be programmed to work at the optimal speed for a given plant. Limiting human work in hazardous environments, because manufacturing jobs often place workers at more physical risk compared to a lot of other industries. Lowering the level of a hazard presented to employees on the job is attractive to executives to preserve company reputation and minimize potential legal liabilities.

10. Reducing longer working hours

Typically people have to have breaks, get distracted and after time attention drops and pace slows. With a robot it can work 24/7, and keeps running at 100%. Typically if you replace one person on a key process in a production line with a robot the output increases by 40% in the same working hours just because a robot has more stamina and never stops. Robots also don't take holidays or have unexpected days off sick.

11. Increased profitability

By increasing the efficiency of your production process, reducing the resource and time needed to complete it, and also achieving higher quality products, industrial robots can thus be used to achieve higher profitability levels overall, with lower cost per product.

12. Improved working environment

Industrial robots are often used for performing tasks which are deemed as dangerous for humans, as well as being able to perform highly laborious and repetitive tasks. Overall, by using industrial robots you can improve the working conditions and safety in your factory or production process. Robots don't get tired and make dangerous mistakes, neither do they suffer from repetitive strain injury.Due to their high accuracy levels, robots can also be used to produce higher quality products which adhere to certain standards of quality, whilst also reducing the time needed for quality control.Industrial robots are able to complete certain tasks faster and better than people, as they are designed to perform these tasks with a higher accuracy level. This and the fact that they are used to automate processes which previously might have taken significantly more time and resources, means that you can often use industrial robots to increase the efficiency of your production line.

13. Improved Quality Assurance

Few workers enjoy doing repetitive tasks and after a certain period of time concentration levels will naturally decline. This lapse in concentration is known as vigilance decrement and can often lead to costly errors for the business and sometimes serious injury to the member of staff.Robotic automation eliminates these risks by accurately producing and checking items meet the required standard without fail. With more product going out the door manufactured to a higher standard, this creates a number of new business possibilities for companies to expand upon.

14. Increased Productivity

Using robotic automation to tackle repetitive tasks makes complete sense. Robots are designed to make repetitive movements. Humans, also by design, are not. The introduction of automation into your manufacturing process has many different productivity benefits, some of which are shown here.Giving staff members the opportunity to expand on their skills and work in other areas will create a better environment which the business as a whole will benefit from. With higher energy levels and more focus put into their work, the product can only improve, which will also lead to extremely satisfied clients.

15. Avoiding workers need to work In Hazardous Environments
Aside from potential injuries in the workplace, staff members in particular industries can be asked to work in unstable or dangerous environments. For example, if a high level of chemicals are present, robotic automation offers the ideal solution, as it will continue to work without harm. Production areas that require extremely high or low temperatures typically have a high turnover of staff due to the nature of the work. Automated robots can minimise material waste and remove the need for humans to put themselves at unnecessary risk.

Disadvantages to robotic bring to working environment
1. Increase unemployment rate and job loss
On working environment cost increasing aspect, where robots are increasing the efficiency in many businesses, they are also increasing the unemployment rate. Because of robots, human labour is no longer required in many factories and manufacturing plants. They can certainly handle their prescribed tasks, but they typically cannot handle unexpected situations.The ROI of your business may suffer if your operation relies on too many robots. They have higher expenses than humans, so at the end of the day you may not always achieve the desired ROI.
However, robots may have AI but they are certainly not as intelligent as humans. They can never improve their jobs outside the pre-defined programming because they simply cannot think for themselves. Robots installed in workplaces still require manual labour attached to them. Training those employees on how to work with the robots definitely has a cost attached to it.Moreover, robots have no sense of emotions or conscience. They lack empathy and this is one major disadvantage of having an emotionless workplace.Also, robots operate on the basis of information fed to them through a chip. If one thing goes wrong the entire company bears the loss. Where a robot saves times, on the other hand it can also

result in a lag. It is, after all, a machine so you cannot expect too much from them. If a robot malfunctions, you need extra time to fix it, which would require reprogramming.If ultimately robots would do all the work, and the humans will just sit and monitor them, health hazards will increase rapidly. Obesity will be on top of the list. So there are advantages, but there are disadvantages as well. It is the twenty first century and we cannot work without machines.Humans are still considered far more efficient than robots when it comes to decision making powers, handling difficult situations, brainstorming, and generally bringing a sense of emotion and empathy into a workplace. Besides, you cannot rule out the significant role of humans in a business. After all, no machine can replace the human factor 'real employees' bring into a workplace. So, AI can raise unemployment and increase factory or shopping center or office working environment cost when their working environment are applied robotic to replace many workers, then machine electricity expense will also increase. Otherwise, human workers can not spend too much electricity expense in cost aspect.

Whilst industrial robots can prove highly effective and bring you a positive ROI, implementing them might require a fairly high capital cost. That's why, before making a decision we recommend considering both the investment needed and also the ROI you expect to achieve. Often the easiest way to get round this issue is to take out asset finance and the ROI of the robot more than pays for the interest on the asset finance.

This is typically the biggest obstacle that will decide whether or not a company will invest in robotic automation, or wait until a later stage. A comprehensive business case must be built when considering the implementation of this technology. The returns can be substantial and quite often occur within a short space of time. However, the cash flow must be sustainable in the meantime and the stability of the company is by no means worth the risk if the returns are only marginal. Yet, in most instances there will be a repayment schedule available, which makes it a lot easier to afford and control finances. Our downloadable automation payback calculator also has a finance scheme option so you can see how this would work for you.

On job loss increasing aspect, Job loss is by far the most significant opposition frequently brought against the use of robots in the manufacturing industry. Industry workers of all levels, from entry-level to veterans, worry about the security of their employment status, and the ability of their job to be replaced by a robot. This panic is more widespread in this industry compared to others because of the closer immanence of a robot takeover in manufacturing.

Macro effects are another topic that usually comes up with job loss. More "big picture" thinkers wonder how the national, and eventually global economy will be affected when manufacturing workers' jobs are displaced. How can this mass unemployment possibly be compensated for, and how can the robots' presumed success be limited from seeping into other industries. However, increased investment costs are a financial counterpoint to industrial robots, with the idea that manufacturing companies will rack up their debt investing in robotic technology. Firms that do not have the funding might even go bankrupt in an effort to keep up with industry trends rather than continue on with normalized operations.Hence, elimination of a whole labor class would presumably occur a bit of a ways down the road, but the implications of this point are too large not to consider. Bringing in robots to take unskilled labor jobs will place more pressure on the economy, education system, and financial market, just to name a few. The United States has always been associated with the grit and work ethic of its blue-collar workers, and robots are threatening to eliminate this aspect of the human population, with a take over of production jobs.

One of the biggest concerns surrounding the introduction of robotic automation is the impact of jobs for workers. If a robot can perform at a faster, more consistent rate, then the fear is that humans may not be needed at all. While these worries are understandable, they are not really accurate.The same was said during the early years of the industrial revolution, and as history has showed us, humans continued to play an essential role. Amazon are a great example of this. The employment rate has grown rapidly during a period where they have gone from using around 1,000 robots to over 45,000

2. Robotic can not perform better to compare human workers, when they need to work long time in any working environment

Robots need a supply of power, The people can lose jobs in factories, They need maintenance to keep them running, It costs a lot of money to make or buy robots, The software and the equipment that you need to use with the robot cost much money. Robots cost much money in maintenance & repair, The programs need to be updated to suit the changing requirements, the machines need to be made smarter, In case of breakdown, the cost of repair may be very high, The procedures to restore lost code or data may be time-consuming & costly.

Robots can store large amounts of data but the storage, access, retrieval is not as effective as the human brain, They can perform repetitive tasks for a long time but they do not get better with experience such as the humans do. Robots are not able to act any different from what they are programmed to do, With the heavy application of robots, the humans may become overly dependent on the machines, losing their mental capacities, If the control of robots goes in the wrong hands, Robots may cause the destruction. Robots are not intelligent or sentient, They can never improve the results of their jobs outside of their predefined programming, They do not think, They do not have emotions or conscience, This limits how the robots can help & interact with people. Robots can take the place of many humans in factories, So, the people have to find new jobs or be retrained, They can take the place of the humans in several situations, If the robots begin to replace the humans in every field, They will lead to unemployment.

Humans fear robots, Robots inspire two types of fear: firstly, that they might take over our jobs, and secondly, that they could take over the world, Robots will steal our jobs, Robots have the effect of increasing productivity rather than eliminating jobs.Robotics become increasingly present in our everyday life, with household robots, medical, industrial, on production lines, not to mention airports, banks, and hotels, So, Robots may dominate the human species. Robots can operate on the basis of information fed to them through a chip, when one thing goes wrong the entire company bears a loss.The robot can save times, but it can also result in a lag, It is a machine so you can't expect too much from them, If the robot has malfunctioned, you need extra time to fix it, which would require reprogramming, If robots would do all the work, and the humans will just sit and monitor them, health hazards will increase rapidly, Obesity will be on top of the list and less labour at workplaces.

3. Increasing training expense

Whilst industrial robots are excellent for performing many tasks, as with any other type of technology, they require more training and expertise to initially set up. The expertise of a good automation company with a support package will be very important. To minimise your reliance on automation companies you can train some of your engineers on how to program robots, but you will still need the assistance of experienced automation companies for the original integration of the robot.

In recent years the number of industrial robots and the applications they can be used for has increased significantly. However, there still are some limitations in terms of the type of tasks they can perform, which is why we suggest that an automation company looks at your requirement to assess the options first. Sometimes a bespoke automated system may give a better or faster result than a robot. Also, a robot does not have everything built into it, often the success or failure of an industrial robotic system depends on how well the surrounding systems are integrated e.g. grippers, vision systems, conveyor systems etc. Only use good trusted robot integrators to be sure of the optimum results if you do choose to use industrial robots.